El Coyote
THE REBEL

Recovering the U.S. Hispanic Literary Heritage

Board of Editorial Advisors

El Coyote
THE REBEL

Luis Pérez

Introduction by Lauro Flores

Recovering the U.S. Hispanic Literary Heritage

Arte Público Press
Houston, Texas
2000

This volume is made possible through grants from the Rockefeller Foundation and the City of Houston through The Cultural Arts Council of Houston, Harris County.

Recovering the past, creating the future

Arte Público Press
University of Houston
Houston, Texas 77204-2174

Cover illustration and design by Giovanni Mora

Pérez, Luis, 1904—.
El Coyote, the rebel : a nonfiction novel / by Luis Pérez; with an introduction by Lauro Flores.
    p.   cm.
    ISBN 1-55885-296-4 (pbk.)
    1. Pérez, Luis, 1904 — Childhood and youth. 2. Mexican Americans — Biography. 3. Los Angeles (Calif.) — Biography. 4. San Luis Potosí (Mexico) — Biography. 5. Mexico — History — Revolution, 1910-1920 — Personal narratives. I. Title.
E184.M5 P424   2000
979.4'0076872073'0092—dc21   00-020773
[B]

⊗ The paper used in this publication meets the requirements of the American National Standard for Information Sciences—Permanence of Paper for Printed Library Materials, ANSI Z39.48-1984.

First published in 1947 by Henry Holt and Company, New York

0 1 2 3 4 5 6 7 8 9   0 9 8 7 6 5 4 3 2 1

Contents

Illustrations

Luis Pérez, 1904-1962
Oil portrait, artist unknown
(*Courtesy Pamela Ann Phillips*)

Introduction

*"I've learned that fiction based on facts is a true expression of life
and as such it has no plot, no beginning and no end."*

—Luis Pérez, in *Chávez Came Home*

LUIS PÉREZ has long remained a largely unrecognized author in Chicano
literary circles. Accordingly, his first and until very recently only known book,
El Coyote, the Rebel,[1] also has lingered for years as an obscure title, seldom
mentioned by critics and infrequently cited in literary bibliographies or other
reference materials.[2] Yet in 1947, when Henry Holt and Co. first released it,
the book was reviewed in a number of publications, including *Booklist,
Kirkus, Library Journal, Los Angeles Times, Kansas City Star, The New York
Times, The New York Herald Tribune,* the *San Francisco Chronicle,* and others.[3] Without exception (at least none I have been able to locate), this initial
mainstream critical greeting was positive—although in some cases, the praise
was tinged with a degree of condescension. Most reviews praised the author's
good humor and underscored the story's simplicity and charm: "Chiefly valuable for vivid, inside views of the rebels' lives. Style exasperatingly simple"
(Joseph Borome, *Kirkus Reviews* 15:184, March 15, 1947); "*El Coyote* has
much charm, in a minor key, many pictures of engaging Mexican rascals and
a few horrid Americans" (Lorine Pruette, *Library Journal* 72: 806, May 15,
1947); "His story is told in simple style" (*Book Review Digest,* 1947, p. 709);
"His whole book is a study in understatement; and its impact, like everything
really Mexican, is delayed" (Milton Bracker, *The New York Herald Tribune
Weekly Book Review,* June 8, 1947, p. 2).

The quaintness widely attributed to the narrative was accentuated by the
illustrations that appeared on the dust jacket and at the beginning of each
chapter (see page ix). They had been drawn expressly for *El Coyote* by the
renowned children's literature author and illustrator Leo Politi[4]—an aspect
not neglected by the reviewers either: "Mr. Perez writes simply and with a
wealth of humor and good-feeling, a feeling matched admirably by Leo Politi in his many illustrations," wrote Edith James (*The New York Times,* June 22,
1947, p. 24). Will Davidson said:

"Luis Perez writes with simplicity and direct charm . . . . Leo Politi's delightful illustrations fit the tone of the book exactly. It isn't great literature at all. It is just a very warm, personal story that is most pleasant reading" (*Chicago Tribune*, May 25, 1947). A reviewer named Robert Leighton resorted to a gastronomical metaphor: "The Leo Politi illustrations which grace every chapter head have a rare Mexican flavor—a delicious dessert with a most satisfying meal" (*Chicago Daily Law Bulletin*, May 28, 1947, p. 2). This last observation is a telling commentary about a literary "dish"; as Silvia Spitta has argued, "We live and speak and write in surroundings where food is metaphorized continually . . . Culturally, we cannibalistically 'consume' or incorporate other cultures."[5] Once devoured, however, *El Coyote, the Rebel* and its author fell into oblivion.

Some records erroneously suggest the existence of an earlier edition of the text, with the slightly modified title of *Rebel El Coyote*.[6] In all likelihood, however, this mistake reflects one of the various disappointments that Pérez suffered in previous attempts to publish his writings, before and after 1947—a grief he would endure until his death in 1962 and which also appears as a minor thematic thread in one of the unpublished manuscripts he left behind.[7] Perhaps confident that the publication of his first book by Harper and Davies was indeed imminent, the author must have released that information, in good faith, for inclusion in his biographical data. A similar situation would emerge thirteen years after, when T. E. Dikty, an editor with Chicago's Shasta Publishers, sent Pérez a telegram informing him that, while it was "a difficult manuscript upon which to make [a] publishing decision," his next novel, *Chico*, had been accepted for publication.[8] This arrangement with Shasta also went sour, and the writer's second volume did not appear until almost a decade later, posthumously and under the title of *The Girls of the Pink Feather*.[9] To my knowledge, no other critic has ever mentioned this text before; nor has it been cited in any article or listed in any bibliography.

The first (and until now only) edition of *El Coyote, the Rebel* has long been out of print and unavailable to the reading public for nearly half a century. This may explain, in part, the scant critical attention it has received. On the other hand, it is also true that *El Coyote, the Rebel* is a hybrid text; a book halfway between novel and autobiography, as we shall discuss. This, coupled with the mystery that for many years enveloped its authorship, may have exacerbated among critics the difficulty of determining the best manner to approach its analysis.

LUIS PEREZ

EL COYOTE
THE REBEL

Illustrations by Leo Politi

HENRY HOLT AND COMPANY

Title page to the original 1947 edition. Leo Politi's line drawings, for good or ill, emphasized the "picturesque" and "naive" aspects of Pérez's narrative.

In 1984, for example, Luis Leal declared:

No podemos estar seguros del origen del autor . . . A pesar de que el protagonista de El Coyote, *Luis Pérez, lleva el nombre del autor de la novela, existe la posibilidad de que la vida del verdadero Pérez sea enteramente distinta, y hasta se podría suponer que el nombre del autor sea otro, siendo "Luis Pérez" un simple seudónimo. El enigma queda en pie. (12)*

We can not be sure about the origin of the author . . . Despite the fact that the protagonist of *El Coyote*, Luis Pérez, carries the name of the author of the novel, it is possible that the life of the true Pérez may be entirely different; and one could even suppose that the name of the author may be different, "Luis Pérez" being a simple pseudonym. The enigma remains.[10]

In Quest of an Enigma

My acquaintance with *El Coyote, the Rebel* began around 1980. Hoping that the author might still be alive, I made several attempts to track him down over the following decade. All inquiries proved futile. With the dearth of evidence, I too began to suspect that, as Leal had conjectured, "Luis Pérez" might be a mere pen name. My suspicions came to a peak in 1990-1991, when I spent a year at UCLA and redoubled my efforts to locate Pérez or his family. "Luis Pérez" is, of course, a very common name, especially in Los Angeles, which made the task even harder. With no assurances that he was still alive or in the area, I decided to at least try to ascertain his existence and, if possible, his identity.

Armed with the apparently autobiographical details recorded in *El Coyote*, I called the offices of the Los Angeles Public Schools to inquire about any records that a Luis Pérez had graduated from Hollywood High School in 1928. I was told that no information could be released without the authorization of the concerned party: the classic Catch-22.

The administrators of Hollywood High School suggested that I contact Mr. A. Wolfskill, president of Pérez's graduating class; he lived in Los Angeles and still participated in alumni activities. Offhand, however, Mr. Wolfskill could remember no one named Pérez—not an encouraging sign because, he said, the annual student groups were very small and he knew almost everyone. Nonetheless, he offered to survey his yearbooks and call me back. He did so the same afternoon. He had found nothing; no pictures of Luis Pérez, and no listing of his name among those who, for whatever reason, had not been photographed for the yearbook. He had also inspected the group pictures, he told me, including those of the Spanish Club and other organizations to which Pérez might have belonged. Naturally, my curiosity (and suspicion) grew.

Suddenly, I was struck by the observation that Leo Politi and Luis Pérez bore the same initials. Could it be that the author of *El Coyote* was in fact Politi himself? Besides the shared initials and Politi's involvement in illustrating the book, other factors also seemed to indicate that possibility: their proximity in age (Pérez was born in 1904, Politi in 1908), their common place of residence (Los Angeles), and so forth. Moreover, Politi, a prolific and celebrated author and illustrator, had always shown an intense interest in Mexican and Chicano life and culture. This is abundantly demonstrated by the themes and the titles of many of his works, some of which were published in English and Spanish: *Little Pancho* (1938); *The Mission Bell* (1953); *Rosa* (1963); and (especially interesting because of their publication dates) *Pedro, the Angel of Olvera Street* [*Pedro, el ángel de la Calle Olvera*] (1946) and *Juanita* (1948). Ultimately, my suppositions about Politi's possible authorship of *El Coyote* turned out to be unfounded. However, the fact that Politi never responded to the letters I sent him in 1991 in care of the Los Angeles Public Library, which were never returned to me, did nothing to dispel my conjectures at that moment.[11]

Near the end of my stay in Los Angeles, I decided to visit Hollywood High School. A close examination of the yearbooks kept in the school library revealed that Pérez was in fact listed among the students not pictured. His first and last names, however, were slightly altered, appearing as "Louis Perex." This explained, perhaps, why Mr. Wolfskill had failed to locate the entry. Ironically, this change in his first name corresponds to a humorous anecdote in Pérez's book:

The first day in my roll-call room a boy in an army uniform spoke to me and asked, "What is your name?"

"Luis Pérez," I answered.

"Louise?"

"Yes."

"But that's a girl's name."

"No, in Spanish my name is spelled L-u-i-s, and sounds the same as the name used for the American girls."

"That is funny—you should change it. I will call you Louie, for short." (150)

Recalling another brief passage in *El Coyote* where the narrator says "I was assigned to the Hollywood High School ROTC band to play third trombone" (151), I then focused my attention on the pertinent group photographs. I felt extremely rewarded when, suddenly, I spotted Pérez's name among those in the caption of a snapshot of the 1927 ROTC band (see page xiii). There he was, standing in the fourth row: a tall young man in uniform holding a trombone.

Luis Pérez *was* a real person, and apparently his book was grounded on factual information—which, I thought, made it an autobiography. My task, once again, was to try to locate the author or his survivors. Back in Seattle, in 1993, I contacted a friend of mine, a lawyer whose brother-in-law, a former Los Angeles police officer, was now a private investigator in the city. By that time I had located a small item in the 1942 volume of *Who's Who in California*, which further corroborated Pérez's existence. I had not checked any materials prior to 1947 earlier because, frankly, I assumed that before the publication of his book Pérez would not have been a person "worthy of notice." I furnished the P. I. with the information I had, which included the author's last known address in Los Angeles (1125 N. New Hampshire), his wife's name and date of birth, and the name of his stepdaughter's husband (Lt. C. K. Phillips, USN). He was unable to find any leads. The neighborhood where Pérez used to live, he said, was now populated by Russian immigrants. No one knew anything about the writer.

By the end of 1995, I was almost ready to give up. I had tried just about everything. A year earlier I had contacted the U. S. Navy in an attempt to discover the whereabouts of Lieutenant Phillips, who surely by now was retired and receiving a pension. With his initials alone and such a common last name, I was told, it would be nearly impossible to find the right person. Then, all of a sudden, I realized that the information I had been able to gather stipulated that Pérez's wife, Amelia L. Moore, was a native of Nacogdoches, Texas, and that her father's name was Richard A. Moore. By coincidence, one of my former graduate students, Brent Carbajal, was at that time a faculty member at Stephen F. Austin State University, in Nacogdoches. I immediately contacted him and, after explaining the nature of my research, I asked him to see if he could find any members of the Moore family still residing in the area. A couple of hours later, Carbajal called me and said: "Your author, Luis Pérez, is buried here, in the Christian Cemetery of Nacogdoches." With his assistance, I established communication with Mrs. Ann L. Phillips, Pérez's step-daughter, and with her husband, Capt. Charles K. Phillips, now retired and living in the outskirts of Nacogdoches.[12]

BAND

First Row: Bates, Hurtz, Aumack, Boysmith, Webster, Harris, Christensen, Wallace, MacIntyre, Magnus, Tannehill, McCann.

Second Row: Marks, Temple, Altomari, Thomas, Morris, Priester, Carol, Grusd, Hoagland, Nelson, Mr. Jenner.

Third Row: McLeod, Matthews, Bunton, Allan, Harris, Spink, Weldon, Dickerman, Ruttan.

Fourth Row: Green, Harwick, Parker, Heineman, Tilden, Perez, Shelden, Bosche.

Fifth Row: Sullivan, Beckwith, Boyd, Prinz, Lowe, Hunt.

The biographical information and other concrete data that I have been able to collect (see page xv) about Pérez come to dispel conclusively all doubts concerning the identity of the author of *El Coyote, the Rebel*, thereby deciphering the enigma lamented earlier by Luis Leal. In addition, the facts also prove quite valuable for the examination of his works.

Luis Pérez was born in San Luis, Potosí, México, on August 25, 1904. One of the records indicates that he was the son of Ramón Pérez and María Pérez (née Beltrán), while a different source lists his parents as Mauricio Beltrán and María Pérez. If we assume that the pertinent anecdote related by the narrator-protagonist of *El Coyote, the Rebel* corresponds factually to the life experiences of the author—as indeed do most of the other incidents in the tale, as far as can be ascertained—it is clear when, and under what circumstances, he migrated to the United States. One source mentions vaguely that he was educated in the "schools of Los Angeles (Calif.) and Mexico." What we know concretely, as stated above and as ascertained in his book, is that he graduated from Hollywood High School, in Los Angeles, California, in 1928. He attended Los Angeles City College until 1933 and, after a protracted interruption, earned a B. A. from Los Angeles State College in 1956. He married Amelia L. Moore—hence the otherwise cryptic dedication that appears in front of *El Coyote, the Rebel*—and, except for one stepdaughter, Ann L. Phillips (née Cox), he had no children of his own. A Republican and a member of the Lutheran church council, Pérez lived for many years in Los Angeles, where he worked as a translator, and as an instructor of Spanish and Italian at his *alma mater,* Los Angeles City College. Between 1959 and 1960, he also was a teacher, first in Roosevelt and then in Leuzinger High School, in Lawndale, a job he apparently held until his death. During World War II, Pérez served in the U. S. War Office of Censorship, "translating incoming and outgoing letters written in Spanish."[13] He died in Los Angeles on October 21, 1962, and his ashes are buried in the Christian Cemetery of Nacogdoches, Texas, his wife's hometown. More revealing indeed are the autobiographical details included in his book.

El Coyote

In one of the first critical references to Pérez's work, Juan Rodríguez makes a brief mention of *El Coyote, the Rebel*, citing it as "autobiography." Luis Leal, on the other hand, in what is ostensibly the only published article (besides my own) fully devoted to Pérez to date, has referred to this book as a "pre-Chicano forgotten novel" and, deals with the text as a work of fiction. Comparing

Pérez's musical talents were undiminished by his partially missing right-hand ring finger—a distinguishing mark noted in his U.S. citizenship papers—and explained in Chapter 12 of *El Coyote, the Rebel.*

(*Courtesy Pamela Ann Phillips*)

the biographical data of the author with the accounts he incorporates in his book, however, it is clear that his story is in fact a lightly fictionalized autobiography or, *vice versa,* a deeply autobiographical novel.

Both Rodríguez and Leal concur in their assessment of *El Coyote, the Rebel* as an important piece in the Chicano cultural puzzle, one eminently representative of the Mexican-American experience and literary expression of the 1940s—a crucial period of synthesis when previous prose fiction trends crystallized and "began to take a clearly Chicano form," says Rodríguez (71). Leal affirms that the content of *El Coyote, the Rebel* is "without a doubt [set in] a Chicano ambience" (12) and adds that this "is a novel that merits to be included in the history of Chicano narrative. It precedes other novels with similar themes and structure, like *Pocho* and *Macho*" (13).[14]

Using direct, first-person narration and a linear development of the plot, the story of *El Coyote* is organized into thirty-nine chapters and spans roughly twenty-five years in the life of Luis Pérez, the protagonist and, purportedly, also the author of the story. Opening in San Luis Potosí, the protagonist's birthplace, on August 25, 1909, during the celebration of young Luis' fifth birthday, the work proceeds to recount a long series of adventures which carry young Pérez through various points of Mexico and the United States and finally concludes in Los Angeles, California, apparently on Wednesday, December 12, 1934, at the very moment he succeeds in securing his U. S. citizenship. The chronology becomes a bit hazy toward the end and, thus, it is permissible to speculate that Pérez may have deliberately blurred it to endow the events of the last date, which corresponds to the festivity of the Virgin of Guadalupe, with a symbolic value, a narrative stratagem that he seems to employ elsewhere in the book.

As Luis Leal has observed, Pérez frames *El Coyote, the Rebel* within a structure that largely conforms to the paradigm of the picaresque genre. For Leal, in fact, "The most interesting feature of this work . . . is not so much the autobiographical information as the elaboration of the countless picaresque adventures of the hero" (12).

An orphan since birth, Luisito (little Luis) is first put under the care of his maternal grandfather and later in the custody of one of his uncles, Miguel Pérez, who arrives at San Luis Potosí from Douglas, Arizona, shortly after young Luis' fifth birthday party. While the orphanage of the character seems to be an authentic element in the biography of the writer, it nonetheless contributes to the immediate location of the story in close proximity to the sphere of the picaresque. This impression is further reinforced by the romantic and suspect genealogy that the narrator attributes himself through the account referred to him by his grandfather: "Little Luis, your mother's name was María. She was an honest, kind and beautiful Spanish-Aztec woman. . . . Your papá was a young French nobleman" (2).

This is one of those few points where the tale seems to deviate from the facts since, according to one of the records, the last name of both Luis' maternal grandfather and uncle should evidently be Beltrán, not Pérez. Of course, it is conceivable that the biographical documentation may be inaccurate, as it is often the case in situations like this.[15] In any case, the tension between oral tradition and written history, which is also an important ingredient of the book, enters the scene here.

The first action we see the young orphan perform—stealing a piece of cactus candy—also contributes to endowing the narration with a picaresque tenor that will only increase through the development of the subsequent episodes. It is also this innocent and playful act which triggers the initial speech of the grandfather about Luis' parents, thereby leading him to establish the central motif that will become the clarion call for all the actions of the protagonist throughout the entire book: education as the vehicle for individual advancement. "Little Luis, [your uncle Miguel] will be here sometime soon. I intend to have him take you back with him to the United States. I will ask him to give you a good education for my sake, your sake, and for the sake of the Holy Church" (3). A few pages later, the old man's subsequent request to his son Miguel continues this same topic: "Miguel, I want you to take little Luis to the United States and see what you can do for him," to which Miguel, following suit, responds, "I'll take him with me [. . .] I will promise, and swear by the Mexican saints, that we will give Luis the best education we possibly can!" (8).

Later, Luis himself will appropriate this subject and use it as the beacon that guides his actions and all his dealings with the numerous characters he will meet. For example, when he is about to be discharged from the rebel army into which he was recruited three years earlier, at the age of ten, he is interrogated by General Contreras about his reasons for wishing to leave the army, to which he responds by expressing his desire to go "some place where I may be able to go to a school and educate myself" (105). When the General asks him where he would go, Luis predictably answers: "To the United States, my General" (105). Two similar exchanges will take place later, already in the United States, first between Luis and his friend Don Juan, in Douglas, Arizona, when the boy tells his friend: "I would like to get a job somewhere, save money and go to school" (107) and later when he tells Miss Magdalene Smith: "My greatest desire is to save my money and go to a school somewhere. I want to learn something, and

I want to do useful things" (134). The conclusion of the story, and evidently the very outcome of the author's life, corroborates the centrality of this theme.

In conformity with the decision made by his relatives, young Luis abandons his grandfather's home and leaves with his uncle and aunt. The night before his departure, however, his grandfather lectures young Luisito and compels him to promise that he will never forget him or his native land: "Mexico was destined by the gods to be a great country for us Mexicans" (8), states the grandfather. After the child pledges to obey his request, the old man, in a highly symbolic act, proceeds to relate the story of the Aztecs' search for the promised land in compliance with the mandates of their gods, the founding of Tenochtitlan, their capital city, and the origins of Mexico's name and national emblem. It is almost as if this is the rite of preparation that will enable Luis to undertake the journey that will ultimately lead him to a new land and a different culture.[16] The book itself, *El Coyote, the Rebel,* seems to be offered by the narrator as proof that he has kept his oath of memory and devotion to his grandfather and to his native country. In the voice of various characters, similar passages related to Mexico's official and popular history (Hidalgo and the War of Independence, El Cinco de Mayo, Pancho Villa's attack on Columbus, New Mexico, etc.) are intertwined in the narrative at strategic points of the book.

Luis' orphanage as a result of his mother's death at childbirth and his French father's forced abandonment (after he is recalled home by his country) places him first under the guardianship of his grandfather, an old and charming but somewhat ineffectual man. Subsequently Luis falls under the tutelage of a cold and indifferent uncle and a sadistic aunt whose heartlessness and violence are a metaphor for the indifference and brutality of the cruel government, which earlier accused Luis' father of being a spy in order to confiscate the properties and money he had left for the child's education, "leaving the family and me to live from hand to mouth" (2), complains the *abuelo.* This prevailing social situation resulted in the chaos and destruction that engulfed the revolutionary and fratricidal Mexico of that historical moment.

This is the life and psychological scheme that comes to trigger the displacement of Luis Pérez northward and which nurtures his future good disposition to settle in a new country and to assimilate into a new culture. The episodes that come between his flight from his uncle and aunt and his definitive transplantation to the United States, and which cover his adventures as a child-soldier in the Mexican revolution (1910-1917) as well as his initial and temporary visits to Arizona, make the bulk of the story and serve various purposes. One such purpose is further illustration of the anarchy and chaos that reigned in Mexico during the armed phase of the Revolution; another is the development of the humorous, picaresque traits and trajectory of the protagonist.

Pérez's ironic treatment of the blinding confusion that prevailed during the civil war in México is well illustrated in humorous anecdotes recounted in Chapter 9, shortly after he has been recruited into the Contreras battalion when he is barely eleven years old. "Since there was nothing to do but to fight for my country and kill or get killed, I kept digging my trench. At last the bugler blew the call to fire [. . .] and finally the soldiers started shooting aimlessly" (37). The company commander puts his hand on the shoulder of the frightened boy and tells him to balance himself and load his weapon:

> "Shoot!" he commanded.
> "At what, Captain?"
> "*No importa,* shoot!"
> [. . .]
> Soon after we stopped firing, a messenger came running with the news that we had won the battle for freedom. All the soldiers were wild with joy, shouting, cheering and shooting at a few stray birds which were flying over their heads or at any object which served as a target (37-38).

Young Luis, like the rest of his comrades, is just an innocent pawn caught up in a vicious game he scarcely understands. He and his companions have little or no idea about the reasons behind the slaughter in which they were compelled to participate.

Although Pérez's childhood involvement in the armed strife may be true, not all the elements recorded in his account are factual.[17] For example, he claims he was part of the seventh battalion, led by General Contreras, which, he says, fought against the forces of General Morales:

> While the rebel army was recuperating in Hermosillo from the first battle, two self-appointed generals, Contreras and Morales, started quarreling as to who should become the governor of the state of Sonora. These two men, who were fighting for one common cause, divided the army in half, thus creating two revolutionary parties, one called the Contreristas; the other, the Moralistas (45).

The existence of General Morales, and of the Moralistas, is indeed ascertained in the historical records about the revolutionary activities in Sonora.[18] It is dubious, though, whether the Morales chronicled in history books and the one we find in *El Coyote* are the same. On the other hand, my research failed to produce any information about any significant leader named Contreras. I did locate, however, an interesting historical anecdote that comes to beckon the hallucinatory dimensions of the reality lived by Pérez and his contemporaries, one of those magical-realistic tales that often overflow reality itself and which makes Pérez's accounting of the revolution less fantastic or metaphorical than it appears to be at first sight:

> *Había en la ciudad de Ures [Sonora] un músico llamado Manuel D. Contreras, que llegó por el año de 1908 (?) formando parte de la banda militar del 22 batallón. Allí cumplió su tiempo de servicio, y determinó quedarse para dar clases de música [. . .] Al culminar el desbarajuste maytorenista, el ex soldado federal se sintió invadido de un desbordante y fervoroso sentimiento constitucionalista, y se levantó en armas. ¿Contra quién? Era lo de menos (500-501).[19]*

> There was in the city of Ures a musician by the name of Manuel D. Contreras, who arrived around 1908 (?) as a member of the military band of the 22nd battalion. He completed his tour of duty there and then decided to stay and give music classes [. . .] During the high tide of the *maytorenista* melee, the ex-federal soldier was overtaken by an arresting and fervent constitutionalist sentiment, and rose up in arms. Against who? That didn't matter (500-501).

I wonder if Pérez had any knowledge about the musician mentioned in this account. Probably not. Regardless, it is doubtful that the Morales and Contreras mentioned in *El Coyote* may correspond to actual historical figures. Rather, it is my belief that Pérez was attempting to portray here, in a thinly veiled manner, the non-fictional strife between Sonora's strongmen Maytorena and Calles. Their last-name initials, "C" and "M," certainly hint at this.[20]

It is interesting to observe that, while in Ernesto Galarza's life story *Barrio Boy* it is clearly the precariousness and uncertainty of life in revolutionary Mexico that forces the young protagonist and his family to leave for the United States, in Pérez's case one important factor of this equation (besides the constant quest for education already referred above) will be the demand for

Mexican labor that prevailed in the United States during World War I: "They need workers because the American Government is recruiting all the able-bodied young men for the army" (108), says don Juan to his young visitor in Douglas, Arizona.

Although he had previously made several sporadic incursions into the United States, it will be only at the end of 1918, in Chapter 31, that Luis officially enters the country, via Nogales, Arizona, as part of a group of temporary Mexican laborers. The official who examines Luis at the immigration office at Nogales tells him: "Young man, let it be known that you are entering the United States of America to pick cotton and to work as a farm hand for the term of one year. At the end of a year you shall return to Mexico. This is in accordance with the laws adopted by the Department of Labor of the United States" (129). This episode in Pérez's life corresponds accurately to the historical events of that epoch.[21] As M. Reisler has documented in his study, "Between 1918 and 1921 [the Arizona Cotton Growers' Association] imported more than 30,000 Mexicans who entered the country under suspended immigration restrictions"(37). From the Mexican perspective, Aguilar Camín has noted the fiscal and economic crisis that jolted Sonora around that time, and which triggered a serious demographic and financial displacement:

> *A principios de 1916, Sonora era un territorio como no había sido desde las épocas de Gándara, setenta u ochenta años antes: pueblos enteros habían emigrado o estaban en ruinas, los capitales habían huido, los valles antes fértiles vivían en la zozobra y el abandono, la escasez de cereales era crónica, el comercio especulaba ayudado por la misma escasez y por el desastre de la moneda constitucionalista de curso forzoso cuya depreciación se multiplicaba en los estados fronterizos por la proximidad del dólar (424).*

In early 1916, Sonora was a land as it had not been since the time of Gándara, seventy or eighty years earlier: entire villages had emigrated or were in ruins, capital had fled, the formerly fertile valleys languished in anxiety and neglect, the scarcity of grain was a chronic malady, merchants engaged in wanton speculation, aided by that scarcity and the disaster engendered by the forced use of the constitutionalist currency, whose depreciation was aggravated in the border states due to the proximity of the dollar.

Luis is clearly part of that exodus. He does work picking cotton and then, in Glendale, Arizona, herding sheep. But, like many, he does not return to Mexico. In 1920, he is evangelized by a Protestant missionary, baptized in the new faith, and sent to Albuquerque, New Mexico, to attend school. After a two-year stint in the Christian school at Albuquerque, Magdalene Smith, the missionary who brought him into her faith, urges Luis to move to Los Angeles, California, to enroll in a seminary, with the aim of becoming a minister. He arrives in Los Angeles on September 13, 1922, and spends a year in the seminary. There he falls in love with Caroline Olson, a "blue-eyed missionary" ten years his elder, a controversial romance which leads to trouble and results in Luis' departure from the institution in 1924.

Later that year, on September 16, the protagonist meets a sympathetic Spanish teacher who counsels him and helps him to enroll in Hollywood High School. There, as we have seen before, Luis becomes "Louis" or "Louie," joins the ROTC, and plays third trombone in the band. He graduates in June, 1928 and then continues his education in Los Angeles City College, until 1933, events which are all congruent with the actual biography of the author as ascertained in our research.

Given on one hand its plot and theme, a recounting of the travails of a Mexican-born protagonist who migrates to the United States seeking a better lot, and on the other hand its picaresque bent and the obvious factors associated with this genre (such as the highly autobiographical content, the utilization of humor and irony as fundamental ingredients of the discourse, and its deliberate social critique), *El Coyote, the Rebel* can be properly situated in the narrative line of Daniel Venegas's *Las aventuras de don Chipote, o, Cuando los pericos mamen* (1928) and Ernesto Galarza's *Barrio Boy* (1971). Formally, it is unquestionably closer to the latter. The journey of the hero in Venegas' book results in disillusionment—i.e., in the negation of the myth of the United States as the land of plenty and opportunity, the conflict being resolved with the return of the protagonist to Mexico—as Nicolás Kanellos has noted in his introduction to that novel. In Pérez's and Galarza's stories, on the other hand, the main characters ultimately choose to remain in the United States and prepare to fully immerse themselves into a process of acculturation that, in fact, they have already initiated.[22]

For Pérez, this acculturation trajectory has clearly begun when, in the penultimate chapter of *El Coyote,* he meets a newly arrived Mexican man, Pablo Calderón, and cannot help but be shocked by the latter's "atrocious" and "broken" English. Luis' growing discomfort in the face of his compatriot's newly discovered *otherness* is further underscored when he remarks how

Pablo "continued murdering the King's English and misusing personal pronouns" (160). In the epilogue of the book, as a sort of finale to the oath of
allegiance ceremony which formally transforms him into a U. S. citizen, Pérez
concludes his story with a highly symbolic scene which seems to emphasize
that he is definitively on the path to assimilation:

> When I stepped out of the building I happened to glance to the right,
> and high on top of the steel mast the flag of my newly adopted coun-
> try proudly waved with the breeze. As I beheld it, I stood motionless
> in a gesture of reverence. Then, after performing a military salute, I
> walked fast to the parking lot, got into my car, and drove to the bus
> station to meet Dolores (164).

Yet it must be noted that as he is walking out of the courthouse, Luis
meets "a jovial, fat, colored guard," who pats him on his shoulder and says:
"Congratulations, mistah, now you is an American citizen. Yeah, suh—you is
one of us" (164). The operative word here is *us*. His previous experiences—
first with Mr. Benson, the exploitative grower who pays him the net sum of
ten dollars for his labor picking cotton for nearly a year and a half, and later
with the jealous Mr. Mingles and other hypocritical types—have taught Luis
that this is a society in which he does not operate on an equal footing. Who is,
then, the *us* implied in the guard's remark?

This notwithstanding, at the end of the novel all seems to indicate that
Pérez—now on his way to meet his girlfriend, Dolores Ramírez—will soon
marry her and that the tale will conclude with a happy ending. The last sentence of the novel is explicit on this score: "On my way to the station I said to
myself, 'if Dolores will say "yes" to my question, that will be the climax of a
perfect today, and the beginning of a new tomorrow.'" Pérez's decision to
depart from the facts and to suggest the marriage of the protagonist to a Mexican woman—when in fact the author married an Anglo-American—is an
interesting element that on one hand reinforces the fictional character of the
book and, on the other hand, obviously bears additional implications for a
sociological analysis of the discourse in the text.[23]

The Girls of the Pink Feather

In Chapter 24, one of the middle and apparently less important sections of *El
Coyote*, Captain Bojorques takes his young orderly Luis to La Casa del Amor
(The House of Love), a brothel in Agua Prieta, Sonora, in northern Mexico.

Despite the humorous incidents—which include a bar brawl, lots of screaming, and the Madame's grabbing Luis by the collar and hurling him out onto the sidewalk (one more of the picaresque misadventures that abound in the book)—this episode would not be particularly important were it not for the fact that it seems to be the kernel from which Pérez's second book would germinate.

Diametrically opposed to the quaint presentation of his first book, Pérez's second novel, *The Girls of the Pink Feather,* was marketed as part of an "adult reading" series linked only by very suggestive titles and published by Carousel Books, an obscure outlet in North Hollywood.[24] This book appeared posthumously, in 1963. Evidently, Pérez conducted the negotiations and final arrangements for its publication on his deathbed.[25]

While no dates are given, the story appears to be set in contemporary times. It opens in Reno, Nevada, with three characters who (we will learn later) are incidental and almost peripheral to the main plot of the story: Art Chandler, an organized crime figure; Helen, a prostitute targeted for assassination; and Charles "The Avenging Angel" Cooke, the hitman charged with eliminating her. In a story lacking entirely in verisimilitude, and presented much in the style of a minor Hollywood or television mystery, "Angel" Cooke, after a couple of brief sexual encounters with Helen, suddenly falls in love with her and helps her to escape to Guaymas, Mexico. Thus, in the first two chapters these two characters move from Reno to Carson City to Tonopah to Las Vegas and, implicitly, to Arizona and then to El Paso, Texas. The attentive reader will notice that, despite the gratuitous sex scenes inserted here (which never really verge on the pornographic), there is present a naive but deliberate tinge of romanticism.

It is in Chapter 3, however, that the true story begins. The protagonist will be Chico, "the affable foundling . . . discovered during one of the freak Guaymas flash floods" (29) and raised by Juan and Margarita Mendoza, the owners and administrators of the Pink Feather, a colorful brothel in the Mexican port of Guaymas, Sonora. This initial scene, reminiscent of Chapter 24 of *El Coyote, the Rebel,* is set on the birthday of the young protagonist who, like his literary predecessor, will rapidly develop into a sort of *pícaro* figure charged with performing a variety of menial chores for his adoptive parents and the resident prostitutes of The Pink Feather.

Trained as a skilled swimmer by Juan Mendoza de León, his adoptive father, Chico becomes a hero when he rescues a girl from drowning: Linda Williams, a rich, blonde, and blue-eyed American. Naturally, Linda becomes the object of Chico's innocent desire. When the girl's wealthy and generous father decides to reward Chico's heroic deed and informs the Mendozas, through a lawyer who represents him, that "The boy may ask whatever he wished within—" Chico rushes to respond eagerly "I want the girl!" (91). Advised by José Rodríguez de la Cuchara de Plata,[26] the lawyer, that his request must remain within reason and that "possession" of the girl is out of the question, affable Chico smiles and says, "If I can't have the girl, can I study to become a *médico?*" (91).

The rest of the story is fairly predictable. Chico attends the Red Fox Academy at Nogales, Arizona, where he confronts the proverbial negative attitudes toward Mexicans. This notwithstanding, he ultimately succeeds in proving his intelligence, his individual superiority, and his capacity for cultural adaptability: "Chico was making many friends at school. The strange customs of the American people no longer bewildered him. In fact, if he hadn't been so homesick for his parents, and his dream girl, Linda, he could have been very happy in the United States" (103). After a short interval, during which he returns to Guaymas to attend his adoptive mother's death at childbirth, Chico is offered a job in The Red Fly, a restaurant owned by Miguel Villanueva, due mainly to his perfect command of the English language. Villanueva's brother, Tomás, turns out to be a physician living in Los Angeles, California. With Villanueva's help and the last portion of the Williams' reward, Chico is able to attend the University of Southern California (USC) and work toward the completion of his undergraduate degree.

In the concluding six chapters, time is greatly telescoped and the actions pile up in dizzying fashion. Upon the death of Margarita Mendoza, Chico is adopted by Helen (the prostitute of the novel's opening scenes), now the accountant for the Pink Feather (and the new madame of the brothel), and her new husband, Doctor Howard, a colorful, self-expatriated physician from Texas. Juan, after a bout with depression due to Margarita's death, recovers and marries "the widow Calderón." And Chico himself, assuming the role of matchmaker, arranges the marriage of Dolores Pacheco, a reformed prostitute formerly intent on seducing him, to Miguel Villanueva.

In one of the many seemingly capricious twists of the story, Chico's infatuation with Linda Williams is inexplicably discarded. Instead, he quickly falls in love with Celia Contreras, a character abruptly introduced toward the end of the story.[27] Chico, however, is confronted with the necessity of leaving her behind, as he has to move to Mexico City, where he has been admitted into medical school. A group of bandits headed by "The Scorpion," which has appeared sporadically throughout the tale, is reintroduced to aid in the fabrication of a happy ending for the story. Chico, in another heroic act, wounds and captures The Scorpion, and helps to kill the rest of the band, thereby winning the reward money that will allow him to accomplish his dream of transforming the Pink Feather into a clinic, the Mama Margarita Clinica [sic], to serve the poor people of Guaymas. Naturally, both Drs. Villanueva and Howard will be part of the project, as Chico will too once he secures his medical degree in Mexico City.

In the final act of the novel, a truly fantastic twist, a rooster Juan has been grooming for years wins a prize and the money will allow Chico to take Celia with him to Mexico City: "Chico, with this money, you can be a student and have a wife. You needn't be separated from Celia" (160). The happy ending is polished to perfection.

Paradoxically, what begins as a sleazy "adults-only" story unexpectedly turns into a highly moralizing and idealized tale in which justice prevails. Virtue and individual industry triumph over social marginality and determinism; prostitutes reform, marry, and form happy families; alcoholics recover; bandits and other social leeches are killed or put in jail; and the metamorphosis of brothel into clinic is under way. Near the end, when don José, the lawyer, tells Chico, "You are a very fortunate young man blessed by the Aztec god *Quetzalcoatl,*" the protagonist responds with this oration: "My success in becoming a doctor will be due to a constant inner voice which urges me to go on. My turbulent past, the rosy dreams of my future, the fickleness of human nature, the suffering of the downtrodden, and the bleak surroundings and poverty of my country inspire me to push forward despite my many disappointments!" (153) Clearly, this is not an autobiographical novel. Yet the discourse encapsulated in this harangue articulates in a very coherent and powerful manner Pérez's humanitarian concerns and sense of individual motivation. The character's resolute stance in dealing with life's vicissitudes, his energetic protestations against social obstacles and deterministic views, all mirror the elevated confidence, the sense of accomplishment, and the self-esteem of the writer himself.

The same optimistic outlook exhibited in *El Coyote, the Rebel,* which doubtless characterized the vigorous personality of the author, is also found in *The Girls of the Pink Feather.* Unfortunately, the latter work is substantially unaccomplished and inferior to the first. Besides numerous typographical and other errors that attest to the carelessness of the publication, unresolved technical and structural problems detract considerably from any value the novel might have otherwise. One could speculate, as I initially did, that the project was rushed and did not have the appropriate chance to mature enough, for its weaknesses are many and very apparent. Yet Pérez had been negotiating its publication since at least early 1954, as attested by the telegram cited above (see Note 6), and as also reported in the *Los Angeles State College Times* on April 9 of that same year: "Luis Perez, State College's soldier of fortune student, has just had his second novel accepted for publication. It's called *Chico,* and Shasta Publishing House of Chicago has placed it on their list for publication next winter." Interestingly, we also discover in the same notice that "The novel was a product of State's Pacific Coast Writer's Conference, held for the first time last summer under the directorship of Professor Frederick Shroyer of the division of language arts." In other words, Pérez must have received professional advice during the preparation of the manuscript—a fact that renders the deficiencies of *The Girls of the Pink Feather* even more puzzling. It is very likely that the schizophrenia embodied by the book, which oscillates between *roman noir* and fairy tale, may be the result of a clumsy publisher's intervention[28] that attempted to make the novel fit into the mold of the "adult reading" series of which it was marketed to be part. Notably, the synopsis of the story included in the article ignores completely the first part of the book: "*Chico* is the story of a little boy who is brought up in a house of prostitution in Mexico, grows up to become a doctor, and returns to convert the brothel into a hospital."

The Dormant Manuscripts

My contact with Pérez's family proved invaluable. In my first telephone conversation, I immediately found out that he had published *The Girls of the Pink Feather;* I also learned that his wife had kept a trunk with a variety of materials including photographs, newspaper clippings, and every review of *El Coyote* ever published. In addition, I discovered that Pérez was an assiduous writer who had been working on a number of manuscripts before his death, including an elaborate project known by his relatives as *The Twilight of the Gods,* a historical novel based on the life of Hernán Cortés and intended to span three volumes.[29] To date, we have been able to locate two manuscripts with the same title and similar subtitles: *The Conquering God: Based on the Life of Hernán Cortés* (338 pp.), a novel about the conquest of México narrated in the first person, purportedly by Cortés himself; and *The Conquering God: Historical Novel Based on the Life of Hernán Cortés* (309 pp.), which is told in the voice of Rodrigo de Pelayo, one of Cortés' soldiers. Like *Chico/The Girls of the Pink Feather,* these works exhibit Pérez's penchant for a continued exploration of his Mexican past—both immediate and more distant epochs. Using a mixture of fact and fiction, of historical and idealized elements, the author seemed intent on maintaining those vital links to his origins.

Some newspaper articles and other records suggest that Pérez may have worked, and even developed in some measure, other book projects. But no vestiges of them have yet been found. Commenting on the then-recent publication of *El Coyote,* Margaret Lovell noted in the *Los Angeles Collegian,* "Luis has just finished his second book and is working on a third. The second one concerns the Mexican nationalists [nationals?] who came to work in the United States during the war, and the third tells what the Mexican thinks of American tourists." (May 27, 1947) Lovell's latter reference seems to allude to *Chico;* the former may have been a project that Pérez discarded at some point. However, the same work also seems to be the focus of a commentary published seven years later:

> The indefatigable Luis is taking no siesta from writing, however, as he is hard at work on a third book, *Country Without Tortillas,* the saga of the braceros who crossed the border during World War II to help sustain our defense effort by working in the fields and factories of the southwest (*Los Angeles State College Times,* April 9, 1954).

The *braceros* theme falls within the parameters of the immigration experience and still connects Pérez to his past, to his Mexican roots. There is, however, another unpublished manuscript in which the exploration of the Chicano experience proper becomes the central matter. This thematic evolution was perhaps symptomatic of a transformation in the author's social concerns. *Chávez Came Home* (226 pp.) is the romantic and at times humorous tale of Frank Chávez, a Mexican American from Los Angeles who enlists in the army, takes part in World War II, and then returns home only to face the confiscation of his native community's lands by "the righteous members of the 'Housing Administration' of the City of the Angels" in conjunction with "the city fathers" (i). The site of Frank's birth, the notorious Chávez Ravine, is described by the narrator as "a happy little valley where the children were able to laugh and play at will, unmolested, while the adults went about enjoying their chosen occupations, minding their own and their neighbors' business without getting in trouble" (i) until the Los Angeles Housing Administration becomes "alarmed" at the sad condition of the "run-down, termite infested, weather-beaten, squalid shanties" in which "the careless people of the happy hidden hamlet" lived. Purporting a false concern, the authorities determine to expropriate the site with the idea of building "an orderly, dignified, well managed, low-rent public-housing project to serve those who were cleaner than the present occupants of the happy little canyon . . . without taking into consideration the sentiments and emotions of the families of the pleasant community" (i). The project, however falls through and the city management instead sells "the repossessed land to a private baseball impresario to build a colossal monument to a the American sport, so that the inhabitants of other communities may come, for a fee, and hear someone shout, 'Strike one!'" (ii).

In the words of the narrator: "The deal with the city and the baseball impresario became a political embroilment, causing the arrest of Frank Chávez, the son of one of the Mexican-American property owners, who refused to retreat peacefully from his inherited plot of land" (ii).

During one night in jail "Frank had a chance to mentally review his turbulent past, and muster his wits in order to defend himself when the 'Black Friday's eviction rift' trial came about" (ii). This novel, then, is a retrospective view of the events preceding the denouement of the Chávez Ravine case, including Frank's past: his shattered love affair with Conchita Campos, his childhood sweetheart; his heroic participation in the war, during which he finds a dead French woman and her surviving baby girl, Suzette, among the ruins of a bombed building; his romantic pursuit and eventual marriage to Jeanette, Suzette's aunt and only remaining relative. As occurs regularly in Pérez's writings, history, politics, and romance intertwine in this manuscript. An interesting aspect of this novel, as a work left in progress, is that it contains at least three possible endings. Perhaps one day at least some of Pérez's manuscripts will become available to the general reading public.

More than half a century after its birth, *El Coyote, the Rebel* reemerges under the auspices of the Recovering the U. S. Hispanic Literary Heritage project. No longer an enigma, Luis Pérez's life story and narrative work are available to readers and critics. Clearly, they enhance our understanding of Chicano literary history and aid us in our efforts to chart the evolution and transformation of the literature produced by writers of Mexican origin in this country. His works shed light on the the social and cultural experiences of an entire generation of Mexican Americans who lived and worked at a unique historical juncture—a generation that still awaits further study.

Lauro H. Flores
University of Washington
April, 2000

Works Cited

Aguilar Camín, Héctor. *La frontera nómada: Sonora y la Revolución Mexicana* (México: Siglo Veintiuno Editores, 1977).

Falcón, Romana. *Revolución y caciquismo: San Luis Potosí, 1910-1938* (México, D. F. : Centro de Estudios Históricos, Colegio de México, 1984).

Flores, Lauro. "De pícaros y *Pink Feathers:* tras la huella de Luis Pérez, 'El Coyote'." *The Americas Review* (Valedictorian Issue, 1999): 222-240.

Galarza, Ernesto. *Barrio Boy. The Story of a Boy's Acculturation* (Notre Dame: Notre Dame University Press, 1971).

Leal, Luis. "*El Coyote: The Rebel,* novela pre-chicana olvidada," Suplemento Dominical, *La Opinión* 221, Los Angeles, California, Oct. 14, 1984, 12-13.

Reisler, Mike. *By the Sweat of Their Brow. Mexican Immigrant Labor in the United States, 1900-1940* (Westport, Conn.: Greenwood Press, 1976).

Rivera, Antonio G. *La Revolución en Sonora* (México, D. F.: Imprenta Arana, 1969).

Rodríguez, Juan. "Notes on the Evolution of Chicano Prose Fiction," in *Modern Chicano Writers,* eds. Joseph Sommers and Tomás Ybarra-Frausto (Englewood Cliffs, N.J.: Prentice Hall, 1979), 67-73.

Root, Deborah. *Cannibal Culture: Art, Appropriation, and the Commodification of Difference* (Boulder: Westview Press, 1996).

Saldívar, Ramón. *Chicano Narrative: The Dialectics of Difference* (Madison: University of Wisconsin, 1990).

Sommers, Josef, and Tomás Ybarra-Frausto. *Modern Chicano Writers* (Englewood Cliffs, N.J.: Prentice Hall, 1979).

Spitta, Silvia. "The Spice of Life and the Taste of Diversity," in *The Americas Review,* 24:1-2 (1997): 197.

Venegas, Daniel. *Las aventuras de don Chipote, o, Cuando los pericos mamen.* Introducción por Nicolás Kanellos (Houston: Arte Público Press, 1999).

———. *The Adventures of Don Chipote, or, When Parrots Breast-Feed.* Translated from the Spanish by Ethriam Cash Brammer; with a new Introduction by Nicolás Kanellos (Houston: Arte Público Press, 2000).

Wyllys, Rufus Kay. *The French in Sonora (1850-1854): The Story of French Adventures From California Into Mexico.* Berkeley: University of California Press, 1932.

Notes

[1]*El Coyote, the Rebel.* New York: Henry Holt & Co., 1947. Juan Rodríguez brought this book to my attention in 1980-1981, for which I thank him. I believe he was also the first one to mention Pérez, in his article "Notes on the Evolution of Chicano Prose Fiction," included in Joseph Sommers and Tomás Ybarra-Frausto's *Modern Chicano Writers* (Englewood Cliffs, N.J.: Prentice Hall, 1979), 67-73.

[2]The only critic who has previously examined this book in any significant way is Luis Leal, *"El Coyote: The Rebel,* novela pre-chicana olvidada," Suplemento Dominical, *La Opinión* 221, Los Angeles, CA, Oct. 14, 1984, 12-13. My article, "De pícaros y *Pink Feathers:* tras la huella de Luis Pérez, 'El Coyote'," appeared in *The Americas Review* (Valedictorian Issue), 1999.

[3]Clearly, this book was more widely reviewed than J. A. Villarreal's *Pocho* (1959) upon their respective *editio princeps.*

[4]Politi's illustrations had to be omitted from the present edition, as their copyright status is not clear. Mrs. Ann Phillips, Luis Pérez's stepdaughter, seems to recall that Pérez bought them outright from Politi when the illustrator became impatient due to the delays in the publication of the book. However, no relevant documentation was found among Pérez's papers. As reported in two tiny articles published in two different local papers, *Los Feliz Hills News* (Oct. 19, 1950) and Hollywood's *Citizen News* (Dec. 22, 1950), Pérez donated the original manuscript of *El Coyote* together with the original brush illustrations by Politi to the UCLA library. This suggests that Mrs. Phillips' recollection is correct.

[5]"The Spice of Life and the Taste of Diversity," in *The Americas Review,* 24:1-2, (1997): 197. See also, as cited by Spitta, Deborah Root, *Cannibal Culture: Art, Appropriation, and the Commodification of Difference* (Boulder: Westview Press, 1996).

[6]Purportedly issued by Harper and Davies (Los Angeles, 1941). This mistaken information is included in a biographical entry printed in the 1942 volume of *Who's Who in California*, p. 715.

[7]*Chávez Came Home* (226 pp.). This novel is the story of Frank Chávez, a Mexican-American who takes part in World War II and returns home, to Los Angeles, to confront the social injustice perpetrated against his family and the other dwellers of the Chávez Ravine. The twin topics of literary creation and publishing dynamics appear in Chapter 33. This manuscript is also the source of the epigraph to this introductory essay.

[8]The full text of Dikty's telegram, dated February 20, 1954, states: "'Chico' difficult manuscript upon which to make publishing decision. However, definite decision now made to accept manuscript for book publication and accordingly we are planning to feature it in our list. Letter of necessary editorial suggestions will follow in a few days. Congratulations and we look forward to a book which will be financially rewarding for all converned." [*sic.*]

[9]*The Girls of the Pink Feather.* North Hollywood, California: Frimac Publications (Carousel Books), 1963.

[10]Leal's article is cited above in Note 2. Unless otherwise noted, all translations are mine.

[11]Politi died on March 25, 1995. He was 87 years old.

[12]Some of the information I include here was either provided or verified by Mrs. Ann Phillips and her husband, Capt. Charles K. Phillips, in an interview I conducted with them in their home at Nacogdoches, June 11-12, 1996.

[13]This sheds some light on the nature of *Chávez Came Home*, one of the unpublished manuscripts mentioned above.

[14]Interestingly, Pérez conducted the negotiations for the publication of *El Coyote* with W. H. Hindle, the *foreign* editor for Henry Holt and Company.

[15]My efforts to secure pertinent documentation, such as Pérez's birth certificate or baptism affidavit, have been fruitless thus far, despite the assistance I've received from Father Rafael Montejano y Aguiñaga, San Luis Potosí's eminent historian.

[16]Curiously, however, Luis' subsequent journey will trace in reverse the pilgrimage of the Aztecs.

[17]In the episode that recounts the battle of Río Verde, for example, Luis says that one of his fingers was shot off. According to the testimony of his family, the author said this was what had happened to his own right hand and, in fact, some photos verify that part of his ring-finger was missing.

[18]See Héctor Aguilar Camín's account of the activities of Francisco de Paula Morales and his brother, Alberto, in his book *La frontera nómada: Sonora y la Revolución Mexicana* (México: Siglo Veintiuno Editores, 1977), pp. 157-163, 192-195.

[19]Antonio G. Rivera. *La Revolución en Sonora* (México, D. F.: Imprenta Arana, 1969).

[20]The rivalry between José María Maytorena and Plutarco Elías Calles (a future president of Mexico), and their struggle over the governorship of the State of Sonora is legendary and has been amply documented by numerous historians, including Aguilar Camín and Rivera. The fictitious names of Morales and Contreras, and of their derivatively named armies the Moralistas ("the moralists") and Contreristas ("the opposition"), are loaded with a symbolic charge. Pérez's irony and dark sense of humor are evident here in light of the cynicism, absurdities, and fratricidal strife he depicts.

[21]For a good accounting of the importation of Mexican labor into the United States during that time, see Mark Reisler's *By the Sweat of Their Brow: Mexican Immigrant Labor in the United States, 1900-1940* (Westport and London: Greenwood Press, 1976), especially chapters 1 and 2.

[22]For Pérez too, as Ramón Saldívar has proposed about Galarza, "the use of the chronotope of the road is specific, organic, and deeply infused with the ideological implications of his story"(165). As was the case for little Ernie in *Barrio Boy,* the motif of the road also allows young Luis Pérez "to describe the sociohistorical heterogeneity of the culture[s] that [have] nurtured him as a child"(165).

[23]According to Mrs. Phillips, it was agreed (by both Pérez and his editors?) that the story would work better if the protagonist married a nice Mexican *señorita.* It certainly deflected any unnecessary controversy that an Anglo-Hispanic marriage might have raised—especially after the conflict created

by Luis' relatively innocuous liaison with Miss Olson was satisfactorily resolved.

[24]*The Girls of the Pink Feather,* by "Louis Perez" was Carousel Book No. 515, "Complete and Unexpurgated," as announced on the provocative cover. Some of the other titles of the series are *Naked Passions; Sin Club; Fires of Lust; Hollywood Virgin; Virgin for Sale; Sex Circus; Carnival of Lust; The Flesh Market;* and *Sex Doctor.*

[25]Pérez died on October 21, 1962, after a protracted bout with cancer.

[26]"Of the Silver Spoon," literally translated.

[27]Another interesting connection is that the last name of this character, Celia Contreras, is the same one that Pérez gives to the general who commanded the battalion in which Luisito fought during the Mexican Revolution.

[28]According to Pérez family, this was in fact the case. Mrs. Ann Phillips recently informed me that she has now found the original manuscript for *Chico.* Unfortunately, I was not able to examine it before this work went to press.

[29]To date, we have been able to locate two manuscripts with the same title and similar subtitles: *The Conquering God: Based on the Life of Hernán Cortés* (338 pp.), a novel about the conquest of México narrated in the first person, purportedly by Cortés himself; and *The Conquering God: Historical Novel Based on the Life of Hernán Cortés* (309 pp.), which is told in the voice of Rodrigo de Pelayo, one of Cortés' soldiers.

El Coyote
THE REBEL

Luis Pérez

To Amelia

1

On the twenty-fifth of August, 1909, in San Luis Potosí, Mexico, after siesta time, in the middle of the patio of an adobe house, there was a large crowd of men and women surrounding a *señorita* and a *caballero,* who were dancing the *Jarabe Tapatío.* By the side of the crowd there were a little girl and a five-year-old boy imitating the dancers. I was the boy, and the occasion of the fiesta was to celebrate the anniversary of my birth.

After the dance, while the people were applauding, I saw that near my aunt there was a plate of sticky cacti candy. It was to be served later in the evening. But I was hungry for sweets, and when my aunt was busy watching the dancers, I quickly grabbed a big piece of candy and stuck it on the back of my neck. As I was sneaking away thinking that no one had seen me, my grandfather took me by the hand and asked, "Where are we going with that candy?"

"What candy, *Abuelito*?" I asked, trying to look innocent.

"This candy," he said, pulling the piece of candy from my neck and handing it to me. Then, overcome with emotion, with tears rolling down his hollow cheeks, and with several tumblers of pulque in his stomach, he began relating to me and to a few of the guests the fate of my father and mother.

"My son," he began, "you are old enough to know and to understand the sad misfortune which befell your parents. You are beginning a life of misery and must learn to face the truth like a brave little man and a stouthearted soldier of fortune."

To this startling information I was all ears, yet I did not quite understand what my grandfather meant. I was too young to comprehend fully, and besides I was more interested in my cacti candy, the party, my toys, and other gifts which I had received.

"Today you are five years old," he continued, sadly.

While I looked at him, he paused to take another tumbler of *pulque*; then running his stiff fingers through my untidy hair, he proceeded with the conversation in a rather low tone.

"Yes, yes, Luis, five years ago today, during the early hours of the twenty-fifth morning of August 1904, you were born and your beloved mamá passed through that gate which men commonly call death! From that moment on you have been living under my and your aunt's care."

Again he paused, and while he was taking another sip of the fermented liquid, I asked, *"Abuelito,* who was my mamá, and what was her name?"

In a sympathetic manner he answered, "Little Luis, your mother's name was María. She was an honest, kind and beautiful Spanish-Aztec woman. She was young and full of joy. María was always trying to help others and made great sacrifices to console and aid the unfortunate. She was my favorite daughter. Yes—*Luisito*—she was my favorite daughter!"

While he was talking I could see that his eyes were full of tears, and I clumsily tried to wipe them off with my candy-soiled fingers. At the same time I asked, *"Abuelito,* do I have a papá?"

With a deep sigh, he continued, "Yes, *Luisito,* you have a papá, but I don't know where he is now. Your papá was a young French nobleman, who came to Mexico as a minister to represent his country. In the course of time he met your mamá, and against my will she married him. One year after you were born, your papá was recalled to France by his government, and since you were just a baby in arms and without your mamá, he decided to leave you under my care, as you were since the day your mother passed away. He left his property and a large sum of money for your education, but unfortunately the Mexican Government soon found out that what I had in my possession belonged to a Frenchman who was suspected of having been a spy. And that being the case, the authorities lost no time in confiscating everything of value, leaving the family and me to live from hand to mouth."

"And now, *Abuelito,* what are you going to do with me?" I asked.

"Now, my grandson," cheerfully he replied, wiping his eyes and blowing his nose, "I am waiting for my son, your uncle, who is coming from Douglas, Arizona, to visit us."

"What is my uncle's name, *Abuelito*?" I interrupted.

"His name is Miguel Pérez."

"When is he coming?"

"Little Luis, he will be here sometime soon. I intend to have him take you back with him to the United States. I will ask him to give you a good education for my sake, your sake, and for the sake of the Holy Church."

"No, *Abuelito*, I don't want to go with my uncle. I want to stay here with you," I cried, as my grandfather held me in his arms.

By this time the musicians were playing, some of the people were dancing, others singing, drinking, and shouting, which made it impossible for my grandfather to continue with the details of my future.

2

The next thing of any importance that I remember was the arrival of my uncle at San Luis Potosí. His arrival was exciting because the family had prepared a big tamale fiesta to celebrate his homecoming. My grandfather secured the services of a small orchestra in order to make the party more enjoyable. Also, since it was Christmas Eve, my grandfather hung two large *piñatas* from a branch of a tree in the patio for us children to break. The fiesta lasted three days and nights.

The *piñatas* which hung from the tree branch were two oval-shaped earthen jars, handsomely decorated with bits of tinsel and streamers of colored tissue paper. One of the jars was filled with toys, nuts, and candy. The other was crammed with flour.

The object of the Mexican Christmas game is for one who is blindfolded to break the swinging *piñata* with a long stick. After it is broken, all the children scramble to gather up the contents. Each contestant is given three chances to hit the jar, and if he fails, someone else is blindfolded and placed near the *piñata* to continue the game.

Early that Christmas Eve my grandfather, the family, and many friends went to the station to meet my long awaited uncle. About five-thirty in the afternoon, when my uncle and his wife got off the train, the crowd which was gathered there was bewildered on seeing the two Mexicans dressed in clothes that were fashionable in the United States at that time. When my grandfather saw them alight from the first-class coach, he broke through the mass of people and embraced his long absent son, extending also a hearty and courteous welcome to his daughter-in-law, whom he had never seen. After a few minutes of chatter and confusion, the men in the crowd took the baggage and led the guests to the carriages in which we rode to the patio of our house, where the carefully planned celebration was continued.

When we arrived at our ranch, the corral gates were thrown wide open, and as we were entering through the arch of the thick sun-baked-brick wall-fence, the musicians started to play a march. When we were near the center fountain, the orchestra modulated from the march to the Mexican National Anthem. Everybody stood still until the last note was played. When the music had stopped, someone in the crowd shouted, *"Viva México! Viva la Patria!"*

"Viva México!" cried the whole crowd.

"Viva el patron de la casa!" shouted one of the coach drivers.

"Viva! Viva!" continued the throng.

At the end of the many cheers and shouts, the confused murmuring started again, and the *piñata* game began. The first boy who volunteered to try to break the goody pot was my cousin, a lad about my age. He was blindfolded and armed with a long stick and placed in the middle of the crowd. He struck three times, failing to strike either *piñata*. The next contestant was an eleven-year-old girl known as the tomboy of the community. She also lost, never coming anywhere near to the swaying jars. The third one to try his luck was a thirteen-year-old bully boy, who kept saying that he could break the pot at the first blow. After being blindfolded he was led toward the jars. He moved forward, and backwards, from one side to the other, until he thought he was at the right place, then swung his stick and missed the target. The second blow was also unsuccessful, but the third time he struck the *piñata* which was full of flour. He was a sight—covered with it. The crowd hissed and booed. While everybody was laughing at the poor fellow, someone in the gathering shouted, "Let Luis Pérez break the other jar."

"Yes, let little Luis try his luck on the other one," said someone else.

"He is too young," exclaimed one of the older spectators.

But regardless of my age, by popular demand, I was blindfolded and placed in the middle of the ring.

When I was somewhere in the center of the circle drowned by cheers and hisses, I groped my way toward the swinging *piñata*. While I was blindly moving about searching for the decorated pot, I felt the flour under my sandals, and so I knew that I must be very close to my target. Then I stopped, raised the stick and swung it, but in vain. At my action a short silence reigned, but when they saw that I had missed the jar, they hissed and booed, and many of them shouted, "To the right, *Luisito*." "To the left, Luis!" "Get closer, Luis!"

Again I raised the stick—and whack! This time I smashed the

stuffed jar, and in an instant I was flattened to the ground, face downward, with a feeling that everybody was on top of me. In a few moments I heard my aunt's voice calling, "Luis! Where is my *Luisito*?"

"Little Luis is on the bottom!" shouted Juanita, the maid.

After the candy, the toys, and nuts had been gathered up by the children and they had removed themselves from my back, my aunts, my grandfather, and Juanita came to help me up.

"Luis, are you killed?" asked Juanita.

"I think I am shot through the heart," I said, as one of my aunts tried to brush the flour off my face.

The rag which was used to blindfold me was around my neck. One of my sandals was missing; my hair and clothes were full of flour, and my right thigh was badly bruised.

At last I was taken inside the house to be cleaned from head to foot, but in a short while I was out again among the crowd enjoying hot tamales and sweet fritters, and drinking chocolate.

Inside the house, when the party was in full progress, the young women whispered to each other and giggled; everything seemed funny to them. The men drank and talked about the last revolution, the good and the bad points of the Federal Government. I also overheard them agreeing that my uncle was the best-dressed man they had seen in San Luis Potosí for some time.

The first night of the fiesta I danced, sang, and even stood on my head to amuse the guests. Finally, after I had performed all the tricks I knew, I was lulled to sleep in my grandfather's arms by the mournful sound of a clarinet accompanied by tinkling guitars and the melodious strains of other instruments.

3

About three months after my uncle's arrival at San Luis Potosí, my grandfather took the whole family to a near-by park for a weekend picnic.

At the park, after we had eaten the tacos, tortillas, and other foods which my aunts had prepared for the occasion, my grandfather rented a boat. It was a hewn flat-bottomed launch with board benches along the inside to accommodate from six to eight people.

After my two aunts, Juanita the maid, my grandfather, my uncle, and myself were on the rude vessel, my grandfather insisted that he was going to paddle it. So, when everything was ready, he wove jerkingly through the lily-covered lake.

When we were about a mile from the landing place, my grandfather pulled the paddle in and began talking to my uncle. As the boat drifted I saw a cluster of lilies touching the hull of it. I was tempted to grab the flowers, and without thinking, I leaned over.

As I was reaching in the water my grandfather said, "Luis, don't do that!" At the same time he whacked the seat of my pants with the paddle.

When I felt the stinging slap I lost my balance and fell overboard. Immediately one of my aunts shouted, "Take him out! He is going to drown!"

My grandfather calmly replied, "Don't worry, daughter, *Luisito* never drowns. He is a big boy, and he can swim."

"Yes, it is true little Luis can never drown; he can swim. I pushed him in the pond the other day, and he swam out of it," affirmed Juanita.

As my grandfather and the maid were explaining that I could swim, my uncle reached over and fished me out of the water, including the cluster of lilies clutched in my hand.

After I was on land again, my aunts and Juanita removed the wet clothes from my body and wrapped me in a *sarape*, putting me near an open fire to keep warm.

While I was bundled up in the *sarape*, my grandfather said to my uncle, "Miguel, I want you to take little Luis to the United States and see what you can do for him. He is a good boy, and I love him very much, but I'm too poor and old to—"

"I'll take him with me," interrupted my uncle, as he rolled a cigarette.

That afternoon, while my clothes were drying near the open fire, I was placed under my uncle's care. When he assumed the responsibility, he said, "I will promise, and swear by the Mexican saints, that we will give Luis the best education we possibly can! We will be good to him and bring him back every year to see you."

My uncle's intentions pleased my grandfather a great deal, and that same day, in the park, they set the date of our departure.

As far as I was concerned, I was not much in favor of going with my uncle. Even though he had tried to be nice to me, I was afraid of him without knowing why. My aunt, his fidgety wife, reminded me of a frightened mouse. But as I was just a five-year-old boy, I had to obey my elders and await the outcome.

During the afternoon of the day before our leave-taking some of my little playmates, both boys and girls, came to bid me good-by. Many of them said that they wanted to come with me, while others wished that I could stay with them.

A few hours later while I was still playing, my grandfather, who was seated in front of an open fire, called me away from my playmates, saying, *"Luisito*, come to your Abuelito. This is your last night with me."

When I came to where he was seated, he took me in his arms and said, "Luis, I don't want you to forget your grandfather."

"No, no, *Abuelito*, I will never forget you," I replied, as I began playing with his mustache.

"I don't want you to forget your native land either. Mexico was destined by the gods to be a great country for us Mexicans." Then tapping my nose with his finger, he continued, "Don't forget your Mexico, little Luis."

"No, *Abuelito*, I won't forget Mexico either."

Then turning toward the older guests, who were sipping *pulque*, my grandfather, who was fond of repeating traditional legends, said, "A long time ago there used to be in the region of the north a tribe of Indians known as the Aztecs. The gods of these warrior people had promised them a better land in which to live. It was to be larger and more beautiful than the place which they then inhabited. Since the faithful Aztecs always obeyed the voice of their gods, they left their country and came to where the City of Mexico is now, looking for the promised land. The Aztecs were told by their gods that they should build a great city on the site that would be indicated by an eagle, with a serpent in his talons, perched on the stem of a prickly-pear tree. And—"

"Did they find the eagle, *Abuelito*?" I interrupted.

"Yes, *mi chiquito*, they did," he replied, pausing long enough to sip his *pulque*.

Then, turning again to his guests, he continued, "In 1325, after a long and weary trip, the Aztecs arrived at an immense lake dotted with many small islands. There the poor Indians stopped to rest. One day two of the Aztecs went to the lake in search of food, and somehow they managed to cross to one of the near-by islands to explore it. And what do you think?"

"What, *Abuelito*?" I asked, although I had heard him tell the story many times.

After taking another sip of *pulque*, he continued relating the tale to his friends. "There, to the surprise of the two Aztecs, they saw a golden eagle on the branch of the prickly-pear tree, greedily eating a long snake. The Indians, realizing that their god's prophecy had been fulfilled, immediately rushed to their people and told them that they had found the promised land.

"In obedience to the sign, the Aztecs crossed to the island, and there on the spot where the two heralds saw the eagle devouring the reptile, the tribe erected a large temple in honor of their gods. They also built a city which they called Tenochtitlán, which means 'the place of the cactus.'

"The Aztecs were very happy. They inhabited the other islands, and on the lake built many houses resting on piles. Numerous canals intersected the various parts of the city, and in later years they called it Mexitli, after their god of war. The Aztecs enjoyed a great prosperity and happiness under their emperors, but after many centuries, the Spaniards came and reduced the poor Indians to slavery. The conquerors then succeeded in draining the greater part of the lake, converting the land into what is now known as the *Valle of México*. The city of Mexitli was destroyed and rebuilt by the Spaniards who called it *México*. Eventually the name was given to the entire country. And the golden eagle which the two Aztecs saw standing on the stem of the prickly-pear tree became the symbol of our National Emblem."

My grandfather continued sipping his *pulque* and talking with his cronies, and I fell asleep in his lap.

4

The next morning I arose earlier than usual only to find more people gathered around the fireplace waiting for the hour of our departure. Out in the middle of the patio I noticed that there were several groups of young and old men dressed in their best clothes. In one side of the yard there was a guitar and violin orchestra playing popular songs. Near the corral wall, next to the main house, there were several old women dressed in their finest array, smoking cigarettes rolled in corn shucks, drinking coffee, gossiping, and making tamales.

Whatever was happening there that early sunny morning seemed to me to be a feast of joy. The men drank, the young women danced, and the children fought over some odd toy or article which they wished to keep as a token of my farewell party. The dogs barked at stray cats, and some of the blackbirds pecked the ears of my pet burro, whose well-shaped black teats I had sucked in place of my mother's breast. The cares of the day were completely forgotten; the hours quickly passed, and soon we found ourselves on the way to the station. The manner in which we arrived at the depot remains hazy in my mind, but I can well remember being on the train and my relatives and friends waving hats and handkerchiefs, throwing flowers and kisses toward us as the locomotive pulled away. Soon after the train began moving I fell asleep, not waking until very late the next day when we arrived at our first stopover place, Aguas Calientes.

In Aguas Calientes we spent five days sight-seeing, and enjoying the hot spring baths for which the place is well known.

On the sixth day we were again on the train going toward Guadalajara, Jalisco. During the last night of our trip, we were thrown off the wooden benches by a sudden jerk of the train as it came to a standstill. In a few seconds, after the locomotive stopped, three armed men entered the coach, and one of them, waving a pistol in either hand, shouted, "Sirs, pass your purses to us quick!"

As the man spoke, one of the passengers cried, *"Bandidos! Bandi-*

dos!"

When my aunt heard the words "bandits, bandits," she took her purse with their savings and stuck it under my pants, just below my navel. As she was placing the bag she said, "Don't talk."

I was frightened by the unexpected turn of events, and while the commotion was going on I clasped my hands and placed them over the protruding lump on my belly. When the leader of the bandits came near us and looked at my frightened eyes, he asked, *"Muchacho,* do you have money?"

"Yes, sir, I have," I replied, stretching my hand and showing him a fifty-cent piece I had in the palm of it.

My aunt gasped at the action. My uncle looked at me astonished, and the bandit laughed loudly. Then he said, *"Muchacho,* don't be afraid. Here is another fifty cents for you."

As he dropped the money in my hand a pistol shot was heard. The bandits ran away, but soon they were overpowered by some of the men passengers. Before long the train was on its way again, and my aunt reclaimed her money and also took the fifty cents which the bandit had given me. After that I went to sleep, not waking until the next day when the conductor came through the coach calling the name of the approaching city, our destination.

When the soot-stained conductor came to the car where we were seated, he shouted, "Guadalajara, Jalisco! Guadalajara is the next station!" Then, while playing with his unruly black mustache, he continued walking and shouting, "Guadalajara, Jalisco is the next stop. Twenty-five minutes for lunch. Change trains for Colima, for Manzanillo, and for Mexico City."

"Guadalajara is my native city," sighed my aunt, while my uncle dressed me.

5

In Guadalajara my uncle and his family spent the balance of their twelve hundred pesos, which he had earned while in the United States. During my first six months with him and his wife, I was happy. They tried to be kind, treating me quite well. I had a lot of new toys, plenty to eat, and two changes of new clothes. A little later, however, I found that I was in for a "long life of misery," as my grandfather had prophesied. My uncle foolishly squandered his hard earned money. My aunt pawned all her valuable jewels, and when everything was gone we were, as they used to say to each other, *"Pobres otra vez."*

These circumstances affected my aunt so that she became very nervous and moody, which caused her to punish me at the slightest provocation. The situation became so bad that at times it was almost impossible to talk to her. Many times she sent me to bed without supper, quite often with a very painful seat, or a back striped black and blue by a wide rawhide belt.

Things were getting worse and worse every day. My poor aunt was annoyed with everything I did. She never liked the way I held my mouth when I looked at her. My eyes were not of the right color to suit her. My eye lashes were too straight and stubby. My feet were flat, and my arms were out of proportion with the rest of my body. My ears were of the criminal type. My hair was unruly, and she often punished me because I had lice on my head. My lips were too thick and two of my teeth were missing. And the thing that annoyed her the most was the way I used to wipe my running nose on the sleeve of my clean shirt. All in all I was not the right or the pretty baby she would have chosen to have around her.

One morning I awoke with a terrific sore throat Every bone in my body ached. I had chills and I noticed that I had lots and lots of little red spots all over my bony legs, arms, and body. As soon as I saw my aunt I told her about my trouble, but she did not pay any attention to my complaint. She was more interested in plucking her eyebrows and painting her lips than in my painful, spotted body.

About ten o'clock that morning a young servant, came into the house, and I described my illness to her. Very carefully she looked at my face, then looked at my arms, then slowly uncovered me and examined my body and skinny legs. Without saying a word or covering me again, she whizzed out of the house, pulling her skirts almost up to her waist and shouting, "*Sarampión! Sarampión!*"

Within five minutes other women from the neighborhood, hearing the news of my case of measles, came into the house bringing with them hot drinks, salves, towels, and bandages. In a very short time I was well greased from head to foot, and wrapped in old blanket and rags in such a way that I looked like a tamale ready to be cooked.

The day was a very trying one. I sweated like a plow horse. Between my moments of delirium I saw and heard many people who had come to see me, bringing numerous things to be used to cure the measles. By the end of the day I was so weak and so weary that I could scarcely open my eyes.

Three days later I was carefully unwrapped only to find that my body was covered with broken sores. On seeing me in that condition, an old lady exclaimed, *"Dios mío, el muchacho se va a morir!"* At the end of the exclamation, she dropped a puppy which she was holding under her arm and hurried out of the house. A few minutes later, she returned with a lemon, a handful of table salt, a cup of vinegar, and a jar with powdered sulfur. She poured the salt and the vinegar into the sulfur jar; then she squeezed the lemon juice and mixed the compound thoroughly. When the poultice was ready she murmured a Hail Mary, and after making the sign of the cross, she applied the stuff to my sores.

The application of the homemade medicine on my broken skin was so painful that I cried and cried until I went to sleep.

The next day I found myself isolated in a little open adobe shack. There were two mastiffs sleeping at the foot of my bed, which consisted of a grass mat and two old *sarapes* spread on the bare dirt floor. Early that morning my aunt brought me a plate of food and left it by my side, but since I was too weak and sick to move, I was not interested in food. I left it there for the dogs to enjoy.

About ten days later I felt better. I got up and sat in the warm sunshine every day for about three weeks. The mastiffs, who had become my faithful companions, licked my sores in such a manner that in a very short while I was able to romp and play again.

In the latter part of 1910, my uncle and his wife decided to hike across the Mexican country from Guadalajara to a little mining town called Cananea, located in the state of Sonora. The preparations for the trip didn't take long. The personal belongings which my uncle decided to take with us were rolled into three separate medium-sized bundles—one for each of us to carry on our backs.

The load assigned to me consisted of my grass mat, two ragged *sarapes,* three large paintings of saints, and one ten-inch statuette known as *El Sagrado Corazón de Jesús.* I believe that my foster parents sincerely thought I was very fortunate in carrying the saints, because they claimed that the blessed images were going to make the long march very easy for me.

Heretofore I had never disputed or doubted the divinity of man-painted saints, but in the course of the long march, I stumbled on a dead branch and rolled down a rocky hill with the pack of holy images on my back. As I was rolling down over dried weeds, grass, and stumps, my faithful dogs followed me, barking madly. When I finally reached the bottom of the hill they licked my face, arms, and legs, all the while whining joyfully. At the same time my relatives, and others who were coming to Cananea with us, came running to find out what had happened to the precious cargo.

While my uncle was hurriedly unwrapping the contents from my blankets, the women were bitterly scolding me for having been so clumsy and stupid. When my uncle finally spread the *sarapes,* we found that one of the saints had a hole poked through the face; the other two had come loose from the frames, and the statuette was completely demolished. At that time I discovered that *El Sagrado Corazón de Jesús* was made of plaster of Paris, and that my relatives had paid two hundred pesos for the honor of possessing such a miraculous saint. Well—whatever the power of *El Sagrado Corazón de Jesús* had been when it was whole was beyond my understanding. But after the blessed statuette had been broken to pieces, I knew that it had to be put out of my blankets, and I hoped my folks would throw it away. Yet, after a long discussion, it was decided that I should carry the fragments bundled in a large red-figured handkerchief.

After that dramatic incident I was never able to force myself to have faith in cast or painted images. I was very much disappointed in saints in general because they let me roll down the hill like an unprotected log. I even felt that *El Sagrado Corazón de Jesús* was pushing me along.

Something very interesting happened which broke the monotony of the long march to Cananea. Early one morning, while we were resting near a railroad station in a town named Sacualco, my uncle heard that an American railroad company was going to build a new roundhouse. After hearing this news, he went to the railroad office and arranged to get a job for himself and free transportation for his family to the place where the company had its proposed project.

Finally, after a long wait in Sacualco, a freight train came along and we boarded it. We were so happy and so excited over the prospect of our train ride that half of the time we were not aware of what we were doing.

In the excitement of boarding a flat coal gondola, I forgot my bandanna with the broken *Sagrado Corazón de Jesús.* When my aunt discovered that I had left my bundle under the water tank, she gave me ten well-aimed lashes on my seat with the coarse rawhide belt, saying, "Luis, this will teach you to take better care of the blessed saints."

We traveled on the gondola for three days and two nights before reaching Colima, a Mexican seaport, whence we soon embarked on an old ship to sail north to Guaymas, Sonora, where my uncle was to be employed.

The last twenty kilometers of our train ride were the most impressive to me. The reason was that, after we had passed the last one of three long railroad tunnels, my aunt discovered that my face was black with soot. This annoyed her, and so immediately she proceeded to punish me for being dirty and careless. When she was whipping me I said, "Aunt, your face is just as black as mine, perhaps blacker."

Again she took hold of the rawhide belt and let me have three more lashes across my legs, saying, "This will remind you not to be so disrespectful and impertinent to your elders."

To me, the sea voyage was the worst experience of the entire trip.

The vessel on which we sailed, known as *El Terror del Pacífico*, was an obsolete battleship which had been converted into a privately owned freighter. The smell of stale fish, together with the odor of fried salt pork, and the slashing of the waves against the rocking old vessel made me very nauseated. I became so sick that I wished right then and there to die and never to see water again.

At last the swaying ship arrived at Guaymas, but the mining town of our destination was still quite a distance away.

After three monotonous months of hard work in Guaymas as one of the laborers of the construction gang, my uncle honorably earned for us from the American railroad company third-class passes to Cananea, the town of our dreams!

It took four days and a half to make the last lap of our trip, which was uneventful, but quite pleasant to me.

6

Cananea at last! From the distance the mining town looked unusual and picturesque. The houses seemed almost to be suspended from the air, or standing on stilts by the side of the rocky hills. The mountains looked green and fresh, and occasionally one could see across the distant high Sierras a dark gulch that might have been an old sunken tunnel. Some of the near-by hills were dotted with the mouths of small tunnels about which could be seen dumps of multi-colored dirt and boulders. Here and there one was able to distinguish the battered towers of old mining shafts. Both the ore cart and the regular railroad tracks wound from hill to hill, crossing muddy roads and narrow paths which led to the large ore smelters. It was a beautiful picture, and I was fascinated with the town.

A week after our arrival in Cananea we found ourselves building a shack in which to live. We constructed our living quarters out of lumber scraps from the mines and castaway five-gallon tin cans. We also made our furniture out of old boxes and crates, which we collected from the company's commissary. There was plenty of food and we had an excellent start in our new location. My uncle was getting good pay for his work in the ore mines.

In Cananea I had many little jobs to perform. Every morning I had to get up about five o'clock to go to the bakery to get bread and milk for breakfast. Of all my jobs this one I liked the best because many times the bakers would give me bits of somewhat burned or imperfect pastries. Often they would tease me by saying *"Muchacho*, would you like to have this burned loaf of bread?"

"Yes, *señor*, please."

"But, *muchacho*, it is burned."

"I like burned foods of all kinds, *señor*," I would say to them, as I quickly took the offerings from their hands.

On my way home I would eat my burned, or otherwise damaged, pastry, and often to help it along I would take a sip or two of milk. Fre-

18

quently I would over-sip the milk, and when I would reach home my aunt would ask, "Luis! You drank some of the milk, didn't you?"

"Well, ye-ye-ye—"

"Come on! Come on! Don't stall," she would shout.

"Yes, Aunt, I took a very little sip to see if the milk was fresh."

She would get hold of the rawhide belt and say, "This will teach you to mind your own business. It is up to me to know whether the milk is sour or fresh," and she would let me have three or four whacks across my back for sipping the milk.

In spite of the fact that there was enough food at home, I was always hungry, and quite often went to the pantry and stole something to eat.

One day my aunt was going to have company for chicken dinner. When she was out of the kitchen, I happened to see one of the chicken legs floating in the broth. I carefully took hold of the drumstick and went out of the house to a hiding place to enjoy my feast. After I had finished eating my bit of fowl, I knew that my aunt would discover my daring and punish me, and so I thought of a scheme to protect my rump. I placed a piece of cardboard between the seat of my pants and my skin. When the time came for my aunt to serve dinner, she found that the boiled chicken had only one leg. Immediately she shouted, "Luis! Where is the other chicken leg?"

"What chicken leg, Aunt?"

"Don't act so innocent. You know what chicken leg I mean. What happened to it?"

"I do not know, Aunt. I haven't seen it. I do not know what happened to it," I answered.

"Oh, yes you do!" she screamed. "You ate it, didn't you? Didn't you?"

As usual, she was ready to strike me with the rawhide, and so when she asked me the last question, I replied, "Yes, Aunt, I ate *la patita de la gallina*." As soon as I said "yes, Aunt," she lashed me with the belt. This time the whipping was not so bad, but I had to cry and scream to keep from giving my device away. Thank God that she never found out my system because after that I used it frequently with marked success.

Another of my tasks was to go every day to the forest and bring home on my back a gunny sack of wood for the stove. And when I did not go after wood, I had to forage along the railroad tracks to pick pieces of hard coal for the front room base-burner. My greatest trouble in performing these jobs in Cananea was that I did not have enough warm clothes, or decent shoes to wear. In the winter time it used to be very cold, and often, while on my way to the mountains, I would stop at the city dumps to pick up old shoes to protect my feet.

One Sunday morning my uncle called me into the house and said, "Luis, today our neighbor, Don Pedro, is having a little gathering to celebrate his seventh wedding anniversary, and we are invited. While you are at the party, I want you to act like a gentleman and enjoy yourself. Also, while you are here, I must tell you that your aunt and I have decided to send you to the parochial school. We hope to speak to Father Montoya about you either today after mass, or tomorrow when your aunt will take you to confession. We want you to study hard and get book learning. You must also keep on performing the duties that you now have at home."

"Yes, Uncle, I will do all that I can," I replied as we began making preparations to go to mass.

When we were back home, my aunt regretted very much not to have been able to speak to Father Montoya about my education. And while commenting on how well the priest looked in the pulpit preaching the sermon, she said to me, "Luis, I want you to be nice to the padres and the dear sisters; they are such good, saintly people. I am praying to the Lord day and night that you may become a priest some day."

"Yes, Aunt, I too hope to become a priest, in order that I may have the right to pray for your soul, and ask God to forgive you for all the times you have beaten me," I meekly answered.

To that she did not have much to say, but her face turned as red as a bullfighter's shirt. Then turning to my uncle, she said, "Come on, Miguel, let us get ready and go to the party. Tomorrow we shall see about Luis' schooling."

Late that afternoon, after everything was ready, we went to the party, and all that I can remember of that celebration is that there were many pretty *señoritas*, plenty of beer, several cases of Mexican and imported liquors, and a large assortment of cigars, cigarettes, and candy. The best part of the fiesta was that young and old could drink and smoke to their heart's content. Everything was free, and that being the case, I had my share.

I started by drinking a small glass of cognac, followed with a little beer. After that I took a glass of white wine, chased with more cognac and beer. Then I smoked a perfumed cigarette and ate candy. Next I drank a glass of tequila, after which it was necessary for me to hurry to the privy to dispose of all my mixed drinks and from there to bed.

By nine o'clock that night I was still dreadfully sick and that over-glorious fiesta cured me of drinking and smoking for all time.

Since I had a hangover the following day, my aunt could not take me to the church to see Father Montoya. I had to remain in bed for three days and wait until the next Monday to enter school.

When the following Monday came, I found myself shut in a rather dark schoolroom with many little boys and an old nun. My work in the convent consisted of praying, reading, writing, and arithmetic. Three times a day the classes from all the departments were taken to the main chapel to pray to some saint for the redemption of a lost soul or for the salvation of some naughty pupil. I was so undernourished that every time I knelt to pray, I fell asleep saying my Hail Mary's and the Lord's Prayer. As far as I knew, I was doing quite well in my school work, but at the end of my first week, an old, bald-headed padre handed me a sealed envelope and told me to take it to my family. I did so, and soon found that it was my report card for the first week in school. My uncle opened the envelope and looked at the card, but it did not mean anything to him as he did not know how to read. The shock came when a man who was staying with us read the report aloud; then we found that it was a very poor one. As soon as my relatives heard the bad news, they both became enraged and proceeded to punish me for being so stupid. Right after my uncle had finished whipping me, he said to the man who read the card and to my aunt, "I'm going to take him out of school—*él no sirve para nada.*" So right then and there my school career ended, and after that I had more work to do at home.

In the latter part of 1913 my uncle bought two donkeys. My duties then were to go to the forest with the burros and bring two loads of wood for commercial purposes. That was more than I could do alone, and an older boy, who knew my troubles, advised me to leave my family.

One day while we were cutting wood he remarked, "Luis, why in the hell don't you run away from home?"

"Run away from home?" I asked.

"Of course!"

"Why?"

"Because your folks don't treat you right. You should not be beaten by your uncle's wife—she is not your real aunt, anyway. She is mean—she is cruel. She is not human! Look at your ear; she almost sliced it off with the whip. It is bleeding!"

"Yes, I know," I replied, touching my wounded ear, "but I don't think I should run away. I like my folks. It is true that they whip me, but don't all parents beat their children?"

"Certainly not! Anyway, don't be a fool. You haven't got anything to lose—you got everything to gain. You've a future ahead of you, and someday you will thank me for this. Listen to me, don't you want to grow to be a strong and independent *hombre*?"

"Yes, I do, but if I run away from home, where am I going to stay? Where am I going to get food? Who is going to take care of me?"

"That's right!" he mumbled to himself, running his thumb across the edge of his ax. "Where are you going to stay, and who is going to take care of you?"

"It is very easy for you to tell me to run away from my good home, but you cannot tell me where I can find a place to live," I replied to his mumbling.

After a short pause he said, "I know. You can stay at my father's ranch, and you may be able to work there for your food. My old man is a good sport. He won't mind if you come to live there. He needs someone to stay in the camp during the day while he and the other men are in the forest cutting wood. Tonight when you get home unload the burros and feed them, as usual; then sneak out to the sunken well, where I will be waiting to take you to the ranch. Don't fail me."

I followed his advice, and about eight o'clock that evening I was riding with my friend to his father's ranch to work as a camp keeper.

My duties as camp keeper were to help feed the horses and mules, to stay in the camp when the workers were away, and to help the owner or his son to distribute rations to the workers. These tasks went on in

the same manner for six months. Then a team driver's helper became
very ill and I was asked to take his place. His duties were to hitch the
horses, load a long four-wheel wagon with oak and pine logs, and control the brakes on the way to market.

My first experience as brakeman proved to be a sad one. Since I
was not accustomed to hanging by the side of the wagon while it was
in motion, I had a lot of trouble with the brake ropes. The roads were
rough, the horses very slow, and the wagon was old and dilapidated.
After a great deal of effort the driver, whose name was Antonio, and I
finally reached the main highway with our load of wood, and as we
were rolling along he said, "Luis, be very careful with the brakes. That
hill over there is a mean one," pointing to one ahead of us. "Always
keep your brake ropes as tight as you can when going downhill; otherwise the cart might get away from us."

"I will be careful," was my answer, as the horses slowly pulled the
wagon to the top of the elevation.

When we started descending the incline, the wobbly wheels
squeaked and crackled, and the driver shouted at the top of his voice,
"Put on the brakes! Pull! Hold on to them!"

I groaned, sweated, and struggled with the brake ropes until we
reached level ground, and with a sigh of relief I said, "I hope that is the
last hill on our way."

"Yes, that is the last one," he answered, and we continued traveling.

As we arrived near the outskirts of the town, I saw what appeared
to be a battalion of soldiers marching toward us. Antonio, who knew
more than I did about the political conditions of the country at that
time, had told me that General Venustiano Carranza had been elected
president of Mexico, and that everywhere bands of rebels were orga-
nizing to help him to overthrow the old regime. When we came nearer
to the soldiers, whose uniforms were dirty and ragged, Antonio asked,
"Luis, do you see those men coming over there?"

"Yes, who are they?"

"They are rebels of the worst sort. They are horse thieves, and have
no mercy. They insult women, kill innocent children, and hang men!"
he replied, excitedly.

He had hardly finished telling me that they were bandits when we came up to the crowd. Some of the soldiers wore soiled cotton caps, while others wore rusty straw sombreros. The greater part of them wore guaraches, although there were a few who were barefooted. The officers used shoes and leather leggings. Their uniforms were in a better condition than the ones the common soldiers wore.

As we approached the group I saw that one of the faces looked familiar. It was my uncle, dressed in an officer's uniform. As he saw me, he ordered the team driver to stop the wagon, and tried to take me with him. I refused to go, saying that I was working and that I could not leave my job. While we were arguing, another officer, higher in rank than my uncle, came and said to him, "*Señor*, the Mexican army waits for no man. If you want this *muchacho*," poking at my thigh with his shiny sword, "you will have to come and get him tomorrow." Then he shouted a command and the troop continued the march, leaving me in the wagon holding the brake ropes as tight as I could, and gritting my teeth.

"Damn it!" said the driver, "I did not know you had someone in the army."

"Neither did I," was my answer, as we started driving toward our destination.

The next day about twelve o'clock, my uncle appeared, with four fat and well-armed rebels under his command, at the door of the place where I was staying. He asked for me, and as soon as I came to the door he demanded an explanation of my running away from home. When I refused to answer, he commanded one of the rebels to arrest me. Once under arrest, I was placed between the four soldiers; then my uncle ordered them to march me through town to the *cuartel*. Some of the people who saw me marching between the four rebels as if I were a criminal felt sorry for me. Others, who thought it was a joke, laughed and remarked, "Look! Look! That little fellow could not be a big criminal, could he?"

"Why don't you get a wet nurse for him?" shouted someone in the crowd.

Thus I was taken to the *cuartel* for safekeeping, and my uncle ordered my escort to place me under careful watch while I was there.

In the army headquarters the rebels and their women went in and out at will. From one of the rooms along the large hall the beating of drums and the sound of bugles could be heard. In the open patio of the *cuartel* groups of soldiers were cleaning their rifles and mending their antiquated equipment. Near the stables there were women and a few men cooking beans, roasting jerked meat, and making tortillas. Some of the women were washing clothes and others were combing their hair. Next to a hitching post an old *señora* squatted on the ground, delousing her daughter's head. Some of the, stable orderlies were caring for the stolen horses, mules and burros, while the gunners were oiling their old-fashioned cannons. Other men were repairing the ammunition coffers and field wagons.

Just outside of the room in which I was confined a group of rebels was surrounding a cock fight between a red and a black rooster. The men shouted, whistled and applauded. In a few minutes the red fowl was flapping desperately and spreading blood all over the place. Soon he was dead, and the owner of the winning rooster shouted, *"Viva mi gallo!* I have the biggest and the best fighting cock of any man in the Mexican army and if you don't believe me, bring on yours. My rooster will fight any and all of them." Then, holding his rooster under his arm, the man shouted again, *"Viva la Virgen de Guadalupe,* and *viva* my black cock too!"

After the fight some of the men started card games and I was ordered by my guard to get away from the window and go to sleep.

The next day, while I was worrying about my misfortune, a young, well-dressed officer came to see me, and upon entering he said, "Good morning, *muchacho.*"

"Good morning, sir."

"Muchacho—the Mexican rebel army needs men to fight the Yaqui Indians and those who oppose our Government's Reformation." He paused for a while, then continued, "We need men. We want you to come with us."

"But, sir, I am not a man. I am just a boy, and I do not know how to fight. Neither have I knowledge of the use of firearms."

"Ah! *Muchacho!*" With a big smile on his face, he put his hands on my shoulders and said, *"We,* the Law—*we,* the Rebels—*we,* the Government, need young blood in our army! *We* will teach you how to fight. *We* will teach you how to handle firearms and how to make love to the beautiful *señoritas*! You will also wear a uniform like mine."

Then taking his hands from my shoulders he stood at attention, and looking at his uniform admiringly, continued, "Well, *muchacho*, the uniform that you will wear will not be exactly like mine, but I will assure you that it will be a uniform."

Under such promises no boy of my caliber would have thought of missing the opportunity of joining the rebels to learn the secret of shooting a rifle, and to master the art of making love to the beautiful *señoritas*.

That same day, while I was in the recruiting office waiting to be taken to the supply department, there came a countryman and said to the officer in charge, *"Señor* Captain, I want to join the rebel army."

"Good, good," muttered the officer, taking out of his desk some papers. "Your name?"

"Jose Maria Dolores del Bosque—the people call me *Alacrán*."

"Good, good. Your age?"

"I will be twenty-five next week."

"Good, good. Married?" continued the officer.

"Yes, Captain."

"Good, good. Sex?"

"Every night, Captain."

"No, no—are you a man?" smiled the officer.

"Yes, Captain, I have—I wear the pants."

"Muy bien, we need men who wear the pants to fight the Yaqui Indians and those who oppose our Government's Reformation," he replied; then calling an orderly, he said to him, "Take Jose Maria del Bosque and Luis Pérez to the supply department to get their uniforms and rifles."

The orderly stood at attention, clicked his heels, performed a military salute, and then he led us to the supply room.

7

I was almost eleven years old when I was persuaded to join the Mexican rebel army. When I reported on the field for my first army training, I was attired in an ill-fitting khaki uniform. Around my waist and across my shoulders were strapped three double cartridge belts, each filled with two hundred cartridges. My army cap was a little large for my head, but it looked very pretty to me. It had a large brass eagle just over the visor, and above the eagle a small shiny number seven, which denoted that I belonged to the Seventh Battalion. My guaraches were the only thing that really fitted me, and that was because I had made them myself. My rifle was an oversized old-fashioned Mauser. I looked more like a comic character in a burlesque show than a real regimental soldier. When a group of rebels saw me coming along the street, swaying from side to side, carrying the Mauser on one shoulder and dressed in the badly fitted uniform, they laughed aloud and one of them remarked, "Look at that boy; the rifle is bigger than he is."

My comrades' ridicule did not bother me in the least. I was very well pleased with the way things had turned out. I was especially thankful because my uncle no longer had charge of me. I was also happy because I had a real rifle, a uniform, plenty to eat, a charming girl friend, and a place to sleep.

For the first two weeks everything went on rather smoothly. At night the army band played in the park. The soldiers carelessly strolled through the narrow walks arm in arm with their wives, sweethearts, or perhaps their mistresses. On Sunday afternoon there were bullfights, and all through the week we, the soldiers, had bull's meat for dinner. The bullfights usually started at about two in the afternoon and lasted until five-thirty or six.

The first bullfight that I saw was held in the Plaza de Toros, which was a great circular building constructed with heavy planks and two-by-fours. The interior was an immense amphitheater, with seats rising in tiers to the top, where the private boxes were located. Half of the seats were shaded by awnings and large palm leaves. The private boxes were in the shadow and very well located, enabling the spectators to see in every direction. The ring, an arena about a hundred and fifty feet in diameter, was encircled by a high fence with several lower barriers on the sides. These barriers served as a means of protection to the men who took part in the show when they were chased by the enraged bulls.

About two o'clock, an hour before the fight, I sneaked in the Plaza de Toros following a group of army officers and soldiers who were detailed to keep order while the bullfight was on. By this time the plaza was becoming filled, and the crew of bullfighters were getting ready to perform their act. And while the hustle and bustle of the people went on, I managed to get a seat near the bullfight committee's box. The committee was composed of several prominent citizens and army generals.

About a quarter to three a bugle corps flourished a resounding fanfare, and right after that a richly dressed *caballero*, mounted on a spirited white horse, entered through a gate which was directly in front of the box where the committee was seated. The *caballero* rode straight toward the committee's box; then, removing his big sombrero and giving a slight salute, he asked the chairman of the committee for the permission to kill the bulls.

The chairman politely bowed, granting the request; then he tossed to the *caballero* the ribbon-decorated key to the bull pen. Unfortunately, the horseman failed to catch the key in his big sombrero, and because of his clumsiness, the crowd roared and hissed him. As he was being hissed, he rode a little distance away, then spurred his white charge, and, coming toward the key in great speed, he swooped down in a very gallant manner and grabbed the attached ribbon. As he performed this unexpected act the hisses were changed to cheers and bravos. While the *caballero* was riding to one side of the ring, a bugle blast brought in thirty marching bandsmen, dressed in colorful uniforms, playing the Toreador's Song from the opera *Carmen.* The band was followed by two gaily dressed matadors. Behind these were eight bullfighters arrayed in costumes of red, yellow, green, and blue silks, satins, and velvets, glittering with beads, jewels, and gold braid. Behind the bullfighters came four men known as the *banderilleros* or dart stickers. Each of the *banderilleros* carried a pair of barbed darts about two feet long with coverings of fancy colored paper, and with ribbon streamers hanging from the handle end. The *banderilleros* were followed by the picadors, who were mounted on old horses. After the picadors came the bull ring assistants, some driving mule teams and others pushing wheelbarrows. Finally, when the procession had marched around the arena once, the band stopped in front of the committee's box and played the Mexican National Anthem, and everybody there sang the words. As the band finished playing, a great *"Viva la Virgen de Guadalupe!" "Viva México!" "Viva la Revolución!"* resounded through the huge wooden amphitheater. After the noise had died away, the band continued the march and went out through the same gate by which they had entered. The Plaza de Toros was full to capacity. The bullfighters took their places and the picturesque setting was ready for the much-advertised performance.

When the band was out of the arena and the gates closed, the horseman who had received permission to start the bullfight appeared in the ring on foot and went to a balcony which was above the gate to the bull pen. At the sound of the trumpet he flung the gate wide open. The bull rushed out from the dark stall into the dazzling light, furious with rage, and trembling in every limb. As the animal was passing through the gate of the stall, a bull ring assistant planted on his shoulders a barbed steel hook covered with flowing ribbons. It was a tense moment for everybody, and all eyes were centered on the beast. Startled by the bright light and enraged by the pain caused by the steel hook, the bull stood for an instant pawing the earth and tossing dust over his back. Around him in the ring were bullfighters carrying red cloaks, and the picadors, who sat like statues upon their steeds, which were blindfolded to prevent them from seeing their danger. The picadors held the horses' reins in the left hand, and in the right, a long blunt-pointed lance.

After a moment of hesitation, the bull dashed at one of the blindfolded horses, and the rider tried to plant his spear into the bull's shoulders, but he missed, and the enraged beast overthrew both the horse and the picador in a heap. As the feast of fury took place the crowd shouted almost simultaneously, "Save him! Save him!"

Immediately, with red capes the bullfighters distracted the bull's attention from the prostrated picador, whose iron armor was pinning him to the ground. Soon the bull ring helpers removed the helpless rider and his gored horse from the arena, and the show continued.

While the fight was in full force the crowd shouted, whistled, and applauded, and drank tequila, which had been illegally brought inside the Plaza de Toros.

After the dart stickers had performed their well perfected act of planting the decorated barbed darts on the bull's shoulder, the bugle corps brought a handsome matador into the arena. His name was Arturo Gaona, but the people knew him as *El Pirata*. Arturo came in through the gate where the band had made its exit, and he walked directly to the chief's box and said, *"Señor presidente de la comisión,* I will kill the bull to the honor of the Mexican Revolution, and to the beautiful *señoritas,* eh?" Then he threw his bullfighter's hat to a pretty girl who was in one of the boxes. When he had finished his speech, he walked to the center of the arena in the midst of hisses, cheers, and hand-blown kisses.

Gaona was a perfect specimen of man. His features had the appearance of being chiseled by a master sculptor. The women admired him and I envied him.

Once in place and ready to perform his act, he waved several times a four-foot staff, which had a red flag pinned from end to end. At his waving of the staff the bull charged at him with all his might. When the beast was almost over the matador who was coaxing him, he saw that the bull was a perfect target. Then, without moving, the stouthearted fellow raised his sword and plunged it up to the hilt into the bull's shoulders.

At this well-performed act, everybody shouted, "Bravo! Bravo! Long live brave *El Pirata!*"

In the meantime the blood gushed through the open wound of the dying bull, and slowly oozed from his mouth and nostrils, while Gaona went around the ring taking bows. The people, wild with joy, cheered, whistled, applauded, and threw hats, coats, cigars, handkerchiefs, and flowers to him. Some of the *señoritas* blew handfuls of kisses to the matador.

The bull ring assistants came in with their gaily decked mule teams and hitched them to the dead bull. As the carcass was being dragged around the ring, someone in the crowd shouted, "Give the tail of the bull to *El Pirata* to honor him for being a good matador!"

"Yes, give him the tail! He deserves the tail! He is a good matador, give him the tail!" echoed other voices.

The *caballero* who had entered the bull ring at the beginning of the performance appeared from somewhere with a huge machete in his hand. He chopped off the bull's tail and handed it to *El Pirata*, who accepted it with much reverence, kissed it, then tossed the souvenir to the girl to whom he had thrown his bullfighter's hat.

The crowd cheered as the well-dressed *señorita* was splashed with blood when the hairy token fell on her. While the mule teams continued dragging the tailless carcass around the arena, the bloody places were covered with sand to prevent slipping and in order to get the ring ready for the next bull.

Once again the bugles sounded the call. There was perfect silence for a moment, and then the new bull came rushing out of the stall, snorting. Again the people went wild with joy on seeing the infuriated brute. The animal stopped. The bullfighters walked closer to him, waving their red cloaks, and thus the second performance began.

After a few rounds with the bullfighters, the picadors, mounted on their blindfolded steeds, came and performed their act to perfection. These men were followed by the dart stickers, who skillfully planted their decorated barbed darts in the bull's shoulders. By this time the beast was enraged and ready for the matador. Arturo Gaona came out. The crowd cheered him. He took a bow, then walked to the center of the arena. The bull charged at him with all his might. The matador performed a graceful move, spreading his red cloak as the animal went by. The crowd cheered at the act. The bull stopped and then charged again, this time goring the man in the ribs and throwing him down into a heap. The crowd became hysterical. The bullfighters came from behind the barriers to coax the bull away from the matador. A man with a medical kit rushed to the wounded man. Then followed two men dressed in white and bearing a stretcher. In the meantime the bull was furiously charging at the bullfighters, but suddenly the beast turned aside and butted a wooden barrier which had a red cloak hanging over it. The thrust was so terrific that it snapped off his two horns. The brute fell to the ground and remained there for some time. Then an army officer came, gun in hand, and shot the suffering animal. As that was done the crowd shouted, "Shame! Shame! Shame!"

The teamsters brought their mules and dragged out the bull. Then the president of the bullfight committee stood in the middle of the arena and shouted, "Ladies and gentlemen, it grieves me to the heart to announce that our brave Arturo Gaona—*El Pirata*—is dead!"

As the people heard the word "dead," the buzzing of voices started again, and all around me I could see men and women making the sign of the cross. Again the president of the committee shouted, "Ladies and gentlemen, the bullfight is over for the day!"

The crowd rushed out of the Plaza de Toros, crying and praying for Gaona's soul. The body of the matador was removed on the stretcher while the band played a slow sad march. Then I went to my *cuartel* making a vow to myself that I wasn't going to see another bullfight as long as I lived.

8

That same Sunday, after eating supper, I went to the park to hear the band play. Across from the bandstand, on the lake, there were several boatmen singing to their customers while they paddled their flower-decorated flat-bottomed boats. I enjoyed the music and the sight of the gondoliers under the moonlight, and temporarily forgot the unfortunate result of the bullfight.

During a band intermission I wandered among the crowd, and I overheard a group of men talking about a girl, who, it seemed, had been the toast of the town, before entering a convent. A farmer who was carrying a big machete said to a soldier who showed signs of having had too much tequila, "Friend, Cananea is not what it used to be. It's gone to the dogs since Rosita Gonzales entered the convent."

"Rosita Gonzales too went to the dogs when she met that young padre who came from Mexico City," replied the drunken soldier.

"Careful, *señor*, don't speak bad of Rosita Gonzales; she is a good *señorita*," retorted the farmer.

"She is not a good *señorita*—she went to the dogs too," continued the intoxicated soldier.

"I am telling you, *señor*, not to speak bad of her, because I will use my machete on you and cut your tongue right out!"

"I don't care, but Rosita Gonzales went to that convent in order to be near that—"

Whack! The large knife sliced off the soldier's ear, and also made a gash in his neck.

Immediately some of the soldiers and policemen took charge of the man with the sharp steel. While they were handcuffing him, he said to the wounded soldier, "Excuse me, friend; I am sorry I missed you. I meant to cut off your head so you won't be able to speak bad about young ladies—especially Rosita Gonzales."

Soon the wounded man was carried to the hospital; his assailant was dragged to jail, and the band concert continued.

The following day, which was Monday, I was present at a court-martial trial. When the tribunal was ready, two armed soldiers delivered a man in chains. As the prisoner stood near a provisional bench, the officer in charge stated, "Don Ramón Mirabosque, you were caught after ten o'clock last night spying in our headquarters among our soldiers. You are accused of wearing a stolen uniform, and for that you are going to be punished. Do you have anything to say before you are sentenced?"

"Yes, my *Commandante*, I do. I want justice!"

"Justice for what?" shouted the officer.

"*Señor Commandante*, your soldiers have burned my house; they stole my horses; they killed my cattle; they trampled my corn field, and they have taken my wife," pleaded the man in chains.

"For you I feel very sorry, Don Ramón Mirabosque, and since you have lost everything and have nothing to live for, I—the com*mandante* in charge of this court—sentence you to be shot at sunrise tomorrow morning," affirmed the *commandante*.

The soldiers were ordered to take the prisoner away, after which another two soldiers delivered another guilty man.

The second culprit was the farmer who had attacked the drunken soldier the night before. When the prisoner was in front of the bench, the officer read the charge of assaulting a member of the Mexican rebel forces with a deadly weapon. The criminal pleaded guilty, and the *commandante* sentenced him to serve three years in prison.

The soldiers were ordered to take the prisoner away; then the com*mandante* dismissed the court, and I went back to the army headquarters to clean my rifle.

9

A week after I joined the Mexican army, my captain commander came to me and said, "My lad, I am very proud of you: As far as I know you are the youngest rebel in the Mexican army. I admire you for it."

"Thank you, Captain," I replied.

"Go and get your Mauser and put on your campaign sombrero, and come back here."

"Yes, my Captain," I answered, obeying his command.

When I had exchanged my army cap for my big straw campaign hat, I got my Mauser, and then I reported to the captain. When we were near the training field he said, "Put your Mauser against that century plant and stand in front of it. I want to take a picture of you to use in the recruiting posters."

I obeyed him, and after he had taken several views of me, he added, "Anyone who will see the picture of the youngest rebel in the Mexican army will be inspired, and they will join us at once."

"I hope so, Captain," I replied, as I went back to the armory room to clean the dust off my rifle.

I never knew what happened to the pictures for the posters, but what I know is that after two weeks of fiestas and daily drilling at Cananea, my regiment was ordered to mobilize at a camp near Guaymas, Sonora, with the object of fighting some of the last scattered Mexican Federal Troops. As soon as the urgent orders were given we entrained for Guaymas, and since the trains in Cananea were at our command, we had no trouble in mobilizing right away. We traveled continuously, and within four days we were near the proposed battlefield waiting for further orders. While waiting I tried to locate my uncle, but I was unable to find him. Later on I was informed that he had deserted the rebels.

In our new camp, the troops were divided into three large companies. The division to which I was assigned was ordered to attack through the center, while the other two were ordered to protect the flanks. The afternoon of the day set for the attack, the entire army was assembled, and the general in command, with the help of the company commanders, read some rigid rules for the benefit of those who did not know the penalty for desertion. At the same time we received orders to be ready to attack the enemy at three o'clock the following morning.

When the corpulent general commander was reading the rules from a military manual, I became so nervous that at that moment I wondered whether to take a chance and desert the rebel army, or to face the enemy fighting like a man, so that perhaps someday, if I came out alive, I might become a great commander such as my general. At the same time everything seemed like a dream, and I had the thought that only three weeks before that nerve-wracking day I had been a free *muchacho*. I felt very bad about the whole matter, but since I had been caught between two trying circumstances, I finally came to the conclusion that the best thing for me to do was to encounter the enemy like a brave soldier and fight for truth, liberty, romance, and—what? Yes— what? That is still a question in my mind today. In reality I never knew what I was fighting for, and I don't believe that the other soldiers did either. While I was thinking about all those things, my captain commander came close to me and whispered, "Luis, my boy, control yourself! Don't be afraid. Be brave like our general! And in the battlefield stick close to me so that in case you get killed, I can bury your body."

"Thank you, my Captain. I shall try to be close to you so that in case you get killed before I do I shall do the same for you," I answered, clicking the heels of my flat-soled guaraches.

"Ah! You are a brave *muchacho*, and I shall always remember you as the youngest rebel in the Mexican army—and one of the bravest!"

I thanked him for the compliment, and as I was performing another military salute, he stepped back and gave orders to his company to get ready for the proposed march to the battlefield.

As soon as we were dismissed, we began rolling packs and filling our canteens with water. Some of the soldiers started to make tortillas and fry beans for their dinner, but the captain told them not to cook because we were going to receive two cans of sardines and a package of soda crackers as our ration for that afternoon.

It was a cold and cloudy evening, and very depressing. In the course of our march to the battlegrounds, it started to rain. I was more frightened by the thunder and lightning that night than ever before—or since.

At midnight the bugler blew the assembly call. At twelve-thirty the general gave the command to march to the front. From the moment the command was given until the end of our march, we heard nothing else but an undertone mumbled by two sergeants, who mingled the "One! Two! One! Two! Left! Right! Left! Right!" with the sound of thunder, rain, and the beat of a muffled drum. The thunder was so terrifying that at times I did not know whether it was cannon shots or only tempestuous explosions.

By three o'clock of that morning we were in our small, badly dug trenches, soaked from head to foot, waiting for the zero hour. Time seemed to drag, and my impatient heart beat so fast that I was afraid it would break through my weak chest.

I was so frightened that I even thought of killing myself, thus getting it over once and for all, but a hidden voice would always stop me, saying, "Don't do it! If you kill yourself you will not go to heaven. If you blow the top of your head off, your comrades will brand you as a coward and not as a hero. Face the enemy! Fight! Fight!"

Since there was nothing else to do but to fight for my country and kill or get killed, I kept on digging my trench. At last the bugler blew the call to fire. Our artillery started the shooting; then the machine guns answered the attack, and finally the soldiers started shooting aimlessly. The first three or four minutes of the fight I was shaking like a leaf. My company commander, who was beside me, put his hand on my shoulder and said, "Steady yourself and load your rifle."

"Yes, m-m-my Captain!" I stuttered.

After I had my Mauser loaded with four bullets in the magazine and one in the barrel, I told him that I was ready.

"Shoot!" he commanded.

"At what, Captain?"

"*No importa*, shoot!"

I closed my eyes, pulled the trigger—and shot! Wow! What a shot! It was one that I will never forget. The kick of my enormous firearm was so terrific that it threw me out of my trench. My captain, who saw the incident, shouted, "Stupid! Get that rifle and shoot it like a man, not like a brainless *muchacho*. Brace the butt against your shoulder, and don't close your eyes when you pull the trigger."

With a "Yes, my Captain," I recovered my Mauser, followed directions, and shot it from time to time until about ten o'clock that morning, when the bugler blew the call to cease firing.

Soon after we stopped firing, a messenger came running with the news that we had won the battle for freedom. All the soldiers were wild with joy, shouting, cheering and shooting at a few stray birds which were flying over their heads or at any object which served as a target.

I felt so big and so proud after the battle that I ran back to my dugout, and smeared mud on my face and hands in order to gain recognition from the soldiers. The first rebel who saw me with my mud make-up laughingly asked, "Where have you been, *muchacho*? Were you with the pigs, or were you fighting?"

"What do you think, soldier? If you think that our captain is a pig, then I am forced to tell you that I was with the pigs; but if you respect him as a fighting man, then I must tell you that I was with a fighting man!"

Other soldiers who heard the conversation started to laugh, and one of them shouted, "Long live the brave Captain!"

"*Viva el muchacho enlodado!*" shouted another.

Still another shouted "*Viva México!*" as he unloaded his rifle at a buzzard, which was eyeing a dead horse.

Thus we marched toward the city, ready for another adventure. By noon we were looting the captured city, making love to the beautiful *señoritas*, drinking tequila, taking possession of live stock, and, in general, enjoying the spoils of war. The following morning at sunrise some prisoners were shot.

Two days after the battle, our battalion was assembled for roll call to find out how many soldiers we had lost. There were twenty of our men missing, but we found only two dead bodies and five wounded men.

After we had given our dead military funerals, we were ordered to camp at the outskirts of the city until further notice. While we were in the new camp, my comrades gave me another name.

10

When the Mexican army was stationed in some large town or city, the men were provided with raw commodities, and they usually took their rations to a boarding house, where a very small amount was paid to the management to have their food cooked. However, when the regiments were in campaign, the soldiers had to prepare their own meals. While we were waiting for further orders in the open field camp where I was properly nicknamed, some of the soldiers complained that the rations which we had received only two days before were not enough for fighting men. The food issued to each soldier for one week consisted of a small bag of uncooked beans, two cups of granulated sugar, a small piece of brown sugar, a cup of *pinole*, a cup of raw coffee, half a cup of rice, about three pounds of flour, and a pound of jerked meat.

One afternoon, while a discontented and hungry sergeant named Pancho was roasting a piece of jerked meat over an open fire, he called, *"Muchacho! Muchacho!* Wake up! I got something to tell you."

"What is it, Sergeant? What do you want?" I asked from beneath my *sarapes*.

"Come over; I got something to tell you. I want you to do me a favor."

"What? I suppose you want me to lend you money again, don't you?" I asked, joining him and some other rebels who were playing poker.

"No, *muchacho*, I don't want your money."

"What is it, then? You are always—"

"The general is going to have a good dinner for himself and the officers," he interrupted.

"How do you know, and what has that to do with me?"

"You shall soon know," he said, looking around to make sure that there were no officers near. "I just came from the general's headquarters and saw the flunkies roasting chickens, and they are making lots and lots of tortillas. A whole pig is being roasted for the feast. I dare

40

you—in fact I *command* you—to go there and steal some of that good food for us."

"Pancho! Are you crazy? I cannot go there and steal food for you just because you send me. I will get shot."

"No, I am not crazy. Captain Felipe Espinosa is in charge of the general's kitchen. He is your captain commander and your friend. If you get caught, you can make the excuse that you came to see him. After you are there—well, you can put some tortillas in the pockets of your coat, and you might even be able to stick a chicken in the bosom of your shirt," he said.

"Yes, *muchacho*, go," agreed one of the poker players.

"Well, Pancho, if you think the plan will work I shall go there and steal food, but if I get killed I will haunt you for the rest of your life," I assured him.

"No, *muchacho*, you will not get killed," he shouted.

The group of rebels laughed uproariously at what I had said to Pancho, and while they were still enjoying the joke I went forth to break the Eighth Commandment.

When I arrived at the place where the flunkies were cooking, one of the guards on duty stopped me, but my friend, Captain Felipe Espinosa, who was in charge of the general's kitchen, saw me coming and commanded the guard to let me pass.

"What are you doing here, Luis, and what are you up to now?" he asked.

"My Captain," I answered, shamefully, "I came to steal food."

"To steal food?"

"Yes, my Captain, to steal food."

"And why, may I ask?"

"Because well—because those roasting chickens over there smell very good," pointing toward the pile of delicious-looking fowls.

"Listen, little fellow," he said, "so long as I am in charge of our commander's kitchen, and so long as you are a soldier in my company, I'll be damned if you will have to steal food from anybody. Come with me."

I followed him to the place where the chickens were and he said, "Here, boy, take this, and this, and this," handing me three roasted chickens and a large pile of tortillas. Politely I thanked him for his generosity and went back to my company.

When my comrades saw me coming with the pile of tortillas on my arm, two chickens in my hand, and the third under my arm, they came running to meet me and immediately wanted to know how I managed to steal so much good food.

"Ah, soldiers of fortune! I always manage to commit a sin, but I never tell how."

They laughed, and one of them took a bottle of tequila out of his pack, and we had a banquet equal to that of our general and his officers. After we had finished eating our sumptuous meal, one of the rebels loudly belched and said, "*Panza llena corazón contento.*"

Pancho rebuked him, "You should not say, 'Full belly happy heart'; rather, we should say, 'Long live the boy who stole food for us!'"

Others answered him with many cheers, but the owner of the bottle of tequila, who drank the most, stood up, holding the empty bottle in the air, and shouted, "Yes, *viva el coyote que se robó las gallinas!*"

"Long live the coyote who stole the chickens," repeated Pancho, while three of the men took their guitars and began singing *"La Cucaracha."*

So, from that day on I was known to my comrades as *El Coyote.*

The following afternoon, while I was going across the camp, I met my captain commander. When he saw me, he remarked, "I heard that you have a new name."

"Yes, Captain, they call me *Coyote*, because the soldiers think that I stole the chickens and the tortillas which you gave me yesterday."

"That is a good name for you, *Coyote*," smiled the captain. Then he said, "By the way, *Coyote*, I saw you at church last night."

"Yes, Captain, I was there. Were you there too?"

"Yes, *Coyote*, and did you see the crown that was on the Virgin's head?"

"Yes, Captain, I did see it. It is beautiful."

"A countryman told me that it has fifty-three diamonds and a hundred and twenty rubies imbedded in pure gold. Think, *Coyote*, in pure gold!"

"Maybe that is why it is so brilliant, don't you think, Captain?"

"Yes, *Coyote*, that is the reason," he replied. After looking around he asked, *"Coyote*, can I depend on you to say nothing to nobody?'

"Yes, Captain, I can keep a secret."

"Good, *Coyote*, good; tonight we are going to steal the Virgin's crown."

"But, Captain, I—I—"

"You get the horses ready by eight tonight. You will ride the pinto and I will ride the black one," he interrupted.

"Very well, my Captain," I replied, as he walked away.

By eight-thirty that night the captain and I were outside of the adobe walls of the church orchard. When we were near a small opening in the sun-dried-brick fence, the captain said, *"Coyote*, you keep the horses here and be ready to help me with the loot."

"Yes, Captain, I will be ready. I hope you will be able to steal the Virgin's crown," I said, backing my horse and his against the wall.

"Coyote, I will bring you not only the crown, but the Virgin too," he replied, as he started cautiously across the orchard.

After a while he returned, carrying a large bundle in his arms. Seeing that the bundle he was carrying was the lifeless body of a woman, I exclaimed, *"Carambas*, Captain! I thought you were joking when you said that you were going to bring the Virgin too. Where is the crown?"

"I guess this *señorita* is a virgin, but not the holy one," he replied, putting the body on the ground.

"A *señorita!* What happened, Captain?"

"Coyote, help me to fan her face—I think she has fainted. Then I will tell you."

"Yes, Captain," I answered, fanning the woman's face with my army cap.

"Coyote, I don't want you to tell anybody about this. No one should know what happened tonight."

"No, Captain, no one will know. What happened?"

"When I was near the back part of the church I heard voices near me. Immediately I climbed a fig tree, and took my pistol in hand. After a few minutes I saw some moving figures coming in my direction. When they were close to the tree a masculine voice said, 'My dear Conchita, let us rest a little while under this shade.' The *señorita* didn't want to, but finally both of them came under the tree. When he was putting his arm around her, I lost my footing, and in my excitement to keep from falling I dropped my gun. When that happened, I saw one person run away and the other fall to the ground. Immediately I jumped down from the tree, picked up my gun, and brought the *señorita* here."

"What are you going to do with her, Captain?"

"I'm going to—"

"Oh, my head! It hurts!" interrupted the girl. Then she asked, "Where are you, Pedro?"

"I am Captain Felipe Espinosa," answered the officer.

"Where am I?" cried the girl, becoming hysterical.

"Compose yourself, *señorita,* I will take you to your home. I'm an honest captain."

"Where is my Pedro? What did you do to him? Take me home, you murderer!"

"*Señorita,* I will take you home right away," said the officer, helping her to mount my horse. "You will ride the pinto." Then he asked, "What happened to you, *señorita?*"

"I don't know. I was with Pedro under a tree when something hit my head, and that is all I can remember."

After she was on my horse and the captain on his, he said to me, "*Coyote,* I will see you tomorrow."

"*Hasta la vista,* Captain," I replied as he led Conchita on my pinto, leaving me to have to walk across the cemetery on my way back to camp.

The next morning, when I saw Felipe Espinosa, I asked, "Captain, what did you do with Conchita?"

"Don't talk to me about her," he replied.

"Why not, Captain?"

"She preferred that coward of a Pedro rather than a brave captain; so I left her to him. I shouldn't have bothered with her at all."

"Are we going to get the crown tonight, Captain?"

"That can wait, *Coyote.* We got other things to do at present," replied the officer as he walked away.

Three days after I was nicknamed El *Coyote,* the whole army was ordered to board a freight train back to Hermosillo, Sonora, a town between Guaymas and Nogales.

While the rebel army was recuperating in Hermosillo from the first battle, two self-appointed generals, Contreras and Morales, started quarreling as to who should become the governor of the state of Sonora. These men, who were fighting for one common cause, divided the army in half, thus creating two revolutionary parties, one called the Contreristas; the other, the Moralistas.

I was with Contreras, and I felt very proud of being one of his soldiers. I was ready to fight for the truth, for right, and for the deliverance of the State. I also was eager to fight for the protection of the charming *señoritas*, the old people, the widows, and the children.

One night a week after we came to Hermosillo, when we were getting ready to retire, a soldier exclaimed as he took off his sandals, *"Madre Santísima*, my feet are killing me! That sandy road we crossed today ruined them."

"That is nothing, my friend," replied another soldier, nicknamed *Tecolote*.

"What do you mean, *Tecolote?*" asked the man, rubbing his sore feet with his two hands.

"My friend, when I was living on the farm with my wife, my uncle sent me a pair of shoes from Mexico City. They were beautiful, and I was very proud of them. Once, however, when we were having a dry season, my wife said to me, '*Tecolote*, if it doesn't rain very soon we will lose our corn and bean crop.' 'I know, my little one, but what can we do?' Then the little lady said, '*Tecolote*, pray to the Virgin of Guadalupe for rain. Promise her that if she sends us rain to save our corn and beans you will walk five kilometers with chick-peas in your shoes. One for every day and every night it would rain.' I did not want to do that, but on seeing my food burning up I did what the little woman asked me to do."

"Did it rain, *Tecolote?*" I asked.

"Did it rain?" he repeated. *"Coyote,* it rained six days and seven nights. That meant that I had to put thirteen chick-peas in each shoe. However, that saved our corn and bean crop."

"Did you walk with the chick-peas in your shoes?" I asked again.

"Yes, *Coyote*, I walked five kilometers with thirteen chick-peas in each shoe, and I didn't even get a blister."

"*Tecolote,* you are the biggest liar I have ever heard," said the soldier, who was still rubbing his sore feet. "We should call you *mentiroso* instead of *tecolote.*"

"That is what my wife called me when I told her that I had fulfilled my promise," replied *Tecolote.* "But you see, in my prayer I didn't tell the Virgin of Guadalupe how I was going to put the chick-peas in my shoes. So, after my wife insisted that I should fulfill my promise, I went to the kitchen, cooked the peas, put them in my shoes, and walked five kilometers without getting a blister on my feet." Then, wrapping himself in his *sarape,* he concluded," Good night, little *Coyote.* Tomorrow I will tell you another story."

"Good night, *Tecolote,*" I replied, wrapping myself in my own *sarape,* and then I went to sleep.

While we were peacefully sleeping on the cold floor of our headquarters, the guard on duty at the main gate of the armory woke us with a shout, "*Cabo de cuarto,* General Contreras comes!"

"Battalion! Attention!" shouted the corporal of the guard.

When General Contreras came into our *cuartel,* he addressed the battalion: "Men, I have urgent orders to carry out. We must move out of this town immediately. We have a lot of traitors here and they are plotting against us. We must leave this enemy town by tomorrow morning if we want to remain a battalion of free soldiers! We will have to fight for our flag—for our country—and for the deliverance of the state of Sonora!" After a short pause, he added, "Men, are you with me?"

"Long live General Contreras!" shouted one of the soldiers.

"Hurrah for the chief!" shouted the corporal of the guard.

"Long live Mexico!" answered the sergeant on duty, and immediately after that, the packing started.

By sunrise we were ready to board a freight train to a safer town. Horses, mules, burros, goats, pigs, dogs, cannons, machine guns, children, women, generals, and the willingly kidnapped *señoritas* were all entrained inside of the boxcars, while the common soldiers had to climb to the roof of the cars.

My captain was detailed to choose six men to burn the wooden railroad bridges after our train had passed them, to delay the enemy trains in case the Moralistas should decide to follow us. In the morning, while the captain was choosing his men, he stood near the depot platform and shouted, *"Coyote! Coyote!"*

"Yes, my Captain," I answered.

"Where in the hell are you?"

"Here, my Captain, here on top of the boxcar," I replied, waving my hand.

"Damn you! Why don't you stay around me? What the hell are you doing up there?"

"Nothing, sir."

"Come down in a hurry—we have work to do. Bring your Mauser, your cooking utensils, and your blankets to the caboose. It is going to be our private car."

"Good, my Captain, good," I said while scaling down the car. When I faced him, I added, "I thought you were going to leave me to sleep my siesta on top of that shaky boxcar."

"Coyote, you are always thinking, aren't you? You know damn well that wherever I go, you will go."

"I know that, my Captain, and I am willing to follow you most any place but *al infierno.*"

"What is wrong with Hell? It might be a better place to live than here. There we might be able to find hotter *señoritas* than the ones we are taking away with us."

"Yes, my Captain, we might, but—"

"But what?" he interrupted.

"I doubt it."

"Don't talk back to your superior officers."

"Yes, my Captain."

"Damn you! You get ready and come with me."

"Yes, sir," I said, as I swung my Mauser, utensils and blankets over my shoulders, and followed him.

In the caboose we found three newly appointed generals, perhaps self-appointed, five men chosen by the captain to help to burn the bridges, and ten five-gallon cans of kerosene. Our captain stood in the front end of the caboose and said, "Men, there are two large bridges we have to burn after our train passes over them. One of the bridges is about sixty kilometers from here. The other is at the foot of the steep climb near Rio Verde, the water tank town. From Rio Verde, if everything goes well, we shall go to Cananea where we shall wait for further orders." He paused for a minute, then continued, "José, Pedro, Jesús, Antonio, and Manuel, each of you take a can of kerosene to the rear platform of the caboose, and leave them there until I tell you what to do with them. I want you to study the problem now, and as the train is crossing the bridge, you will pour the oil slowly on the ties." He paused again, then shouted, *"Coyote*, your job is to light these oil-soaked torches and throw them so as to land on the ties and start the fire."

The men took the cans of kerosene to the rear platform, and I took the torches; then simultaneously we chanted, "Yes, my Captain, we shall burn the bridges."

Finally, after a long, unavoidable delay, the heavy train, which consisted of two water tanks, three gondolas loaded with coal, one passenger coach, about twenty boxcars of all descriptions, and a caboose, was slowly pulled from Hermosillo by two regular-sized locomotives toward the first bridge which we were ordered to burn.

11

Our train soon steamed its way through the town of Hermosillo toward Rio Verde. The soldiers who were on top of the boxcars were lazily swinging their sun-baked feet over the edges of the roofs. Others who were less daring sat in the center on the walking boards, playing cards, singing, and drinking.

In the caboose the three newly appointed generals, the captain, and the five men chosen by him were shooting dice. I was in the observation window flirting with one of the charming *señoritas* who was in a cattle car just ahead.

About two hours after our train had started, the captain called us and said, "Men, you'd better get ready. We are approaching the first bridge."

The five appointed rebels ranged themselves on the rear platform, ready to empty the kerosene on the ties, and I was all set to throw my burning torches on the oily timbers.

As we reached the wooden bridge, the captain shouted, "Men—are you ready?"

"Yes, my Captain, we are ready," the men chorused.

"Let it go!" he commanded.

The train slowly crossed the bridge and the soldiers poured the oil on the ties. The captain and I enjoyed throwing the burning torches, which started the fire. Some of the blazing sticks landed very nicely on the timbers, while others fell through the open spaces to the ground below.

Our duty was so well performed that one of the newly appointed generals took from his campaign bag a bottle of tequila and handed it to the captain to compensate us for our good work. Our progress toward the water tank town was very slow because our train was a heavy one. The generals, the captain, and the five men drank the tequila and played cards. I went to sleep.

We traveled all that day and night until about four o'clock the following evening, when the same five soldiers poured kerosene on the ties of the second wooden bridge. The captain and I cast our oil-soaked torches, and in a very short time the old wooden frame was in roaring flames.

At this time the train was creeping uphill. The captain was praising us for our good work, saying, "Men, you have done a damn good job, and I'm proud of you. As soon as we reach our destination we will celebrate the burning of the bridges."

As the captain was talking to us, a clumsy soldier known in the company as *El Zorrillo* decided to come down from the top of the cattle car to the caboose to visit us. While *El Zorrillo* was happily scaling down the iron ladder, he accidentally stepped on the coupling rod, causing the caboose to be disconnected from the main train. Immediately the caboose began rolling backward. As it was gaining momentum, the captain ran to apply the brakes, but the apparatus was complicated, and the captain's efforts were ineffective. The moving caboose was at this point about two city blocks from the burning bridge, and the generals, the captain, and all of us were getting ready to jump.

Jesús, the smartest one of the crowd, took his rifle and wrapped it in his blanket, then ran to the back platform and threw the bundle on the tracks, causing the caboose to derail. Thus we were saved from a flaming grave, but we were badly jerked and frightened almost to death.

The main train backed and picked up the caboose, and all was well again. The only thing we lost in that accident was one rifle, part of a blanket, and one man—*El Zorrillo*—who was shot at sunrise the next morning.

In due time, Jesús, the brightest soldier, was made a captain, though a few days later he complained bitterly, saying that the rank granted him was far below his merit. He claimed that since he had saved three generals, one captain, five rebels, and one *coyote* (meaning me), he should have been made at least a second, if not a first, commander of the entire Contreras army.

12

In Rio Verde we were forced to stop for minor repairs on one of the locomotive boilers. While we were waiting, the enemy overtook us, but a soon as we heard that the Moralistas were coming, we received orders to spread over the near-by hills to fight them. The worst error that we made there was to build our trenches out of loose rocks and heavy boulders. This arrangement was bad because many of the bullets that struck on the top of the rock wall bounced off and hit our soldiers. The enemy cannon also caused us a lot of trouble by showering us with a torrent of flying rocks whenever the shells shattered our trenches. More casualties were caused by wild bullets than by actual aim.

This scrimmage was a sad experience for me. A wild bullet hit the tip of my right third finger, leaving it dangling by only a small bit of flesh and skin. As soon as my captain commander saw my bloody hand, he sent me to the Red Cross for treatment.

The Red Cross was in Rio Verde. In reality, what we called the Red Cross was nothing but a railroad passenger coach converted into a miniature hospital on wheels. A one-eyed doctor and six rather elderly nurses were the only hospital attendants. The seats of the coach were transformed into small beds, which looked quite clean and neat but were very uncomfortable.

When I reached the hospital car, the head nurse came to the door and asked, "What is the matter with you, boy?"

"I do not know, *señora*—I think that I have lost my little finger," I replied, showing her my hand.

"Your hand is all bloody!"

"Yes, ma'am, and it hurts very much."

"Come in, let me see it," she commanded.

Inside the wheeled-hospital, she looked closely at my hand, and after exclaiming, "*Jesús, María y José!*" she remarked, "It is all broken to pieces! It is not your little finger that is dangling; it is your ring finger. How did you do it?"

"I do not know, *señora*. I think some Moralista *cabrón* shot it off."

51

"It looks very bad," she said, then left me there, standing with my bloody hand placed on the other, while she went to the end of the car shouting, "Doctor! Doctor! Where are you?"

"What is it, Esperanza?" answered the doctor from the observation end of the coach.

"We have a patient. Please come over—the lad is bleeding to death!"

While waiting for the doctor, the nurse brought a small pan with warm water and washed my hand. And when the doctor, who had a black patch over his left eye, came, he asked, "What is the matter with you, *muchacho?*"

The nurse, who was carefully drying my hand, answered him before I had a chance to explain my trouble.

"This boy had his finger shot off!"

"Let me see it," said the doctor, taking hold of my hand and examining my finger; then looking at my face he mumbled, "Um-m-m-hum son, it looks bad. We will have to amputate this finger."

"Doctor, do you mean to tell me that you have to cut off my finger?" I asked, chokingly.

"Yes, my son, yes—we will have to amputate it," he repeated.

"When, doctor?"

"Tomorrow, boy, tomorrow," was his answer.

"Why tomorrow, doctor? When my finger hurts very much today! Why don't you cut it off today?" I dared to ask.

"Ah!" Puffing up his chest proudly, he said, *"Muchacho* of the Contreras's army, my profession does not permit me to operate on you today because I have to put you under chloroform, and you must first be cleaned internally."

"Yes, yes," said María.

"Of course!" murmured Conchita.

"Yes, indeed!" echoed Josefina.

"By all means!" agreed Teresa.

"You must, boy, you must!" mumbled Doña Pancha. "It is true, the profession demands that you should be cleaned internally," said the head nurse, affirming what the doctor and the other five helpers, who had gathered around me to see my mutilated finger, had said.

After the doctor had heard the nurses' remarks, he uttered a guttural sound commanding them to put me to bed.

Esperanza, the head nurse, immediately ordered the other nurses to take care of me, and calling them by name, she said, "María, give him a bath. God knows he needs it!"

"Yes, I will, *señora*," said María.

"Conchita, give him half an ounce of castor oil."

"Right away, *señora*," answered Conchita.

"Josefina, inject a dose of morphine in his left arm."

"Yes, *señora*, I'll do so at once."

"Teresa, bring the towels, the pillowcases, and the blankets for his bed."

"Yes, *señora*, I will," murmured Teresa.

To the oldest and homeliest nurse of the five, she said, "Doña Pancha, you watch over him while he sleeps."

"*Con mucho gusto, señora*, thank you. I shall take his temperature every hour," mumbled Doña Pancha, as she sat by my side and held my wounded hand.

"*Diós mío!* Why so much attention all of a sudden?" I asked.

The chief nurse, holding her hands clasped over her big stomach and her head high in the air, haughtily answered, "My little man, the Red Cross is impartial. It does not make any difference who gets wounded, hurt, or killed, the Red Cross treats everybody alike," and then she left.

Everything was performed as Esperanza had instructed, and within twenty minutes the injection of morphine was taking effect in such a manner that my head was feeling very strange and seemed to be going around and around, until I fell asleep.

13

About ten o'clock the next morning I was properly strapped and stretched across a physician's operating table, waiting for the doctor to pour chloroform on a piece of cotton packed inside a towel folded in the shape of a cone. When the doctor finished pouring the volatile liquid on the cotton, he placed the cone over my nose and mouth, saying, "Breathe!"

I did breathe, and—*carambas!* I almost choked to death.

"Again," the doctor commanded.

This time I decided to fool him and took a very short breath, but it was just as bad as the first one. When the physician saw that I had disobeyed him, he angrily, said to me, "Take a long and deep breath. I don't have all the day to waste with you. Don't think that you are the only soldier in the Mexican army. There are other men waiting for my services."

At this rebuke I filled my lungs with chloroform fumes, and this time I really choked myself insensible. As I drew the last breath I felt my head going around and around; and as the sensation of dizziness began, I saw a wide circle composed of many colors coming from somewhere closer to the point between my eyes. When the colored revolving wheel reached the place between the eyes, everything went black, and that was the last of me.

What the doctor and the nurses did when I was under the anesthetic is beyond my knowledge, but the thing I can well remember is that about six in the afternoon, the head nurse woke me from my long forced sleep by pulling the tip of my tongue with an oversized pair of tweezers. As soon as I opened my eyes, the nurse, casting a sigh of relief, said, *"Gracias a Dios, el muchacho vive!"*

"Yes, *señoras*— 'thanks be to God, the boy is alive!'" repeated Josefina, the nurse who had injected a dose of morphine in my arm the day before.

The next thing that happened was the arrival of the one-eyed doctor, who came to my bedside and told Doña Pancha, the nurse who was taking care of me, to get me ready because I was going to be transferred to the main hospital in Cananea. Time was not wasted; so in a very short while I was carefully placed inside a boxcar with other wounded rebels to be taken to the main hospital.

In Cananea I was placed under the care of a group of much younger and more beautiful nurses than the ones I had had before. In fact, some of the new hospital attendants were so charming and vivacious that their mere presence made me feel better right away.

Three weeks later I was well enough to be dismissed from the main hospital, and so the chief doctor ordered me to pack my belongings and report to my battalion for duty.

As soon as I was out of the hospital I made some inquiries as to the whereabouts of the Seventh Battalion, and I was immediately informed that my regiment was about fifty leagues south of Cananea. On hearing of the location of my company I decided to stay in Cananea and enjoy life.

Once away from the hospital and from the drudgery of the army, I felt free. Free to do anything my heart desired. I thought that since I was eleven years old, and since I had had so many thrilling experiences fighting two major battles for the deliverance of the State of Sonora, I should do something about *my* freedom. I also felt that since I had lost one finger fighting for the protection of old people, defenseless children, innocent women, and the amiable *señoritas*, I had a right to my liberty and to call myself a self-made man! With such thoughts in mind I deserted the Mexican rebel army, and went to live with a family whom I had known while living with my uncle in the mining town of Cananea.

14

To desert the Mexican army was an easy thing to do, but to keep from being caught by the rebels was a hard task. A few days after I had deserted I thought I should get out of Cananea and hide where no one knew me. But I wondered and wondered, thinking, "Where am I going to hide, and how am I going to live?" As a whole, it was a gloomy prospect. I had no money, no friends, no family, nor a sure place in which to hide. I noticed that the people with whom I was staying were getting tired of me, and that worried me more than anything else. From day to day I tried to plan a way to get out of trouble, but every proposed scheme that came to my mind failed to materialize.

One day while I was pondering over the possibilities of finding a new home, Don Federico, the man who had provided a hiding place for me the time I ran away from my uncle's home, came to visit the man in whose house I was staying. Don Federico was very much pleased to see me. He asked me a lot of questions concerning my affairs, and when I told him that I had lost a finger in the battle of Rio Verde, he felt bad about it. And when I informed him that I had deserted the rebel army, he felt worse.

"Luis," he asked, "why did you do it? Why did you desert the rebels? Those horse thieves are a bunch of bad *hombres*! If they catch you, they will kill you—and then—what?"

"Yes," I said, "and *then* what? I never thought of that, or I might not have deserted the army. I think I should go and give myself up, for they might have a little mercy on me." Then I reached for my sombrero, and as I was going out, my host arose and took me by the arm, saying, "Don't be a fool! They will murder you!"

"Yes, they *will* murder you!" repeated the visitor.

"Well, then you will have to give me a job on your ranch," I said to Don Federico.

"Ranch! Those damned bandits took every horse, mule, and cart that I owned—I have no ranch," he answered. "I have only a few burros left."

The host spoke, "Don Federico, why don't you take Luis to your place and hide him there until the other party of rebels comes to Cananea."

Don Federico turned to me and said, "Son, you know me. I have always liked you, and I have always wanted to help you, but this time I am afraid. However, if you would like to work with me for a short while, you are welcome to do so, but I will not be responsible for what may happen to you. Tomorrow morning I am leaving Cananea with twenty burros loaded with drygoods, sugar, and coffee to trade in the near-by mining and farming towns for cheese, furs, hides and gold. The job is yours if you want it. I will pay you fifty cents a day and your food. Only one thing I am going to ask of you, and that is that I don't want you to take the job and then leave me stranded on the way with my caravan of burros. I intend to come back to Cananea within a month or so, and after that time you may do whatever you please."

"I will take the job, Don Federico," I said, "but what if the rebels catch me?"

"Well, that will be something that neither you nor I will be able to help," he answered.

Here was an opportunity; so, the next morning I found myself on the back of a saddled burro, helping my master and his son pilot a drove of stubborn beasts loaded with merchandise across the rocky hills and ravines to the first trading post.

The trip was a pleasant one. The only thing that bothered me then was that my wounded finger was not entirely well, and at times it was very painful.

While I was on the trip I ate a lot of green, as well as ripe, wild fruits—pomegranates, figs, crab-apples, pears, prickly-pears, and cherries. I drank plenty of clear running water and slept in the open spaces with a stone or a pack saddle under my head for a pillow, while the mosquitoes hummed me to sleep.

At the end of five weeks we were back at Cananea with a very good cargo of furs, hides, and cheese. Don Federico carried two large pouches of silver coins and three medium-sized flasks of gold dust in his saddle bags. As soon as we arrived at Don Federico's house, we unloaded the burros and put them in the corral, leaving the servants to attend them while we cleaned up a bit to eat the first home-cooked meal that we had had in weeks. The lady of the house called us in for dinner, and when we had finished eating the delicious roasted turkey and other tasty dishes, my master said to me, "My boy, I am quite pleased with your work. We have done very well—in fact, better than I had expected." Then he took from the table a pile of silver coins, which he had carefully counted while we were eating, and continued, "Here are twenty pesos, and I thank you for your help. I would like to keep you here in my house, but to tell you the truth, I am afraid. You are—well—son, you are a deserter, and if the rebels catch you in my house, you might cause me and my family a lot of trouble and grief."

I took my twenty pesos and said to my master, "Don Federico, you have always been very kind and considerate. I will never forget you for all the kindness and favors you have bestowed upon me."

As I addressed him, he offered me his hand, saying, "Good-by, my son! May God bless you, and may the Virgin of Guadalupe keep watch over you!"

"Good-by, master!" I said, as I shook his hand and went forth to wander.

15

With twenty pesos in my pockets I went to visit Don Pablo, the man in whose house I had been staying when Don Federico offered me my burro-driving job. Don Pablo and his wife were very glad to see me. They told me almost everything that had happened in Cananea while I was away. Both of them asked me to stay with them for a week or two if I wished. I thanked them graciously for their kindness, and told them that I expected to leave Cananea the following morning. They insisted on my staying with them at least overnight. I did so, and that evening I had to listen to Don Pablo's hard luck stories of how he lost his job. He said that the rebels had been destroying the railroad lines, and the company stockholders could not afford to keep the mines going in full force. His wife also told me that they were getting very short of funds, and that her son had been spending entirely too much money on the wild *señoritas*. My friends' stories were so sad and pathetic that I felt quite generous and pulled from my pocket ten pesos which I gave to them.

As Don Pablo's wife was putting away the money, he said, "Luis, day after tomorrow all the people of Cananea will celebrate the sixteenth of September." After pausing for a moment, he asked, "Luis, do you know who was the Father of the Mexican Independence?"

"Well—I—"

"Come closer to the light," he interrupted me, taking a book from the bench where he was sitting.

When his wife and I were near him, he said, "The Father of Mexican Independence was born in—let me see—" He paused again; then fingering the pages, he proceeded, "Yes, here we are. 'The Father of the Mexican Independence was born in Guanajuato, Mexico, the 8th of May, 1753.'" Closing the book, he relaxed and continued, "His name was Miguel Hidalgo y Costilla. He was educated in the church for the priesthood and became a well-known and loved Father. He was of pure Spanish blood, but he loved the Mexican Indians. Everybody admired him for his strong and lovable character. He always dreamed of schools and education for the poor. When he was in charge of the church in the Village of Dolores, he established a pottery shop within the premises of the building, and there he met a potter whose name was Pedro Jose Sotelo. One warm evening during the month of August 1810, Father Hidalgo said to his friend, 'My good man, if I were to confide in you a plan of great secrecy, would you guard my trust?'

"'Yes, *señor* Hidalgo, I will take your secret with me to the tomb,' said the potter.

"'Good, keep my secret and listen to me,' continued the priest. 'It is not right that we, being Mexicans, and possessors of such a beautiful and rich country, should remain any longer under the despotic government of the Spaniards. They are robbing us, keeping us under a heavy yoke which we are unable to bear. They treat us as though we were slaves; we are not even permitted to speak as we wish. We have not the right to enjoy the fruit of our own soil. They own everything. We pay tribute to them in order to live in our own country, and you married men have to pay to the Spanish crown in order to live with your own wives. We are, in reality, under a tyrannical oppression. Don't you think that all this is an injustice?'

"'Yes, Father, it is an injustice,' answered the potter.

"'Very well,' continued Father Hidalgo. 'Now, my plan is to overthrow this heavy and hideous yoke. By removing the viceroy and denying obedience to the king of Spain we could become free and independent. But in order to accomplish all this, it is necessary to unite—take up arms—run the Spaniards out of the country and never allow any other foreigner to set foot on our land. What do you think? Would you be willing to follow me and help carry out the plan? Would you die, if need be, in order to liberate your country? You are still young, you are a married man, and you will have children. Don't you think that they should be able to enjoy liberty and have freedom to delight themselves with the products of their homeland?'

"'Yes, Father, I think they should be free,' replied the potter.

"'Very well, guard my secret; don't tell it—not even to your closest friends,' said the priest."

Don Pablo was so excited when he was telling the origin of the Mexican Independence Day that he took off his jacket, unbuttoned his shirt, and kicked off his sandals. Then he stopped long enough to drink a large glass of diluted tequila, after which he went on with the story. "Yes, Luis, that talk was the beginning of the plan to break away from the Spanish oppression. The date for the uprising was set to take place the second of October, during the celebration of the fair of *San Juan de los lagos*, but unfortunately the plan was discovered and betrayed to the government, thus forcing Father Hidalgo and his compatriots to begin their movement before they were thoroughly prepared. In the early hours of the sixteenth of September, 1810, Father Miguel Hidalgo y Costilla began tolling the bell of his parish church in the Village of Dolores, and from the surrounding hills the Indians flocked to the call of their beloved pastor. Word had been spread that great events were impending. When the people had gathered in the church and courtyard, the white-haired curate entered his pulpit, and gazing over the anxious upturned faces of his flock, addressed them for the last time; 'My children,' he said, 'to us this day comes a new dispensation. Are you ready to receive it? Will you be free? Will you make the effort to recover from the hated Spaniards the land stolen from your forefathers three hundred years ago?' And when he had finished his speech he raised his voice and exclaimed, '*Viva La America*! Long live our Holy Virgin of Guadalupe! Long live the Republic of Mexico, and death to the bad government!' The throngs answered him with many cheers after which the priest raised a sacred banner bearing the figure of the Virgin of Guadalupe. Immediately he organized a little army of three hundred men, armed with clubs, swords, knives, and bows and arrows. At the head of these insurgents he marched to Guanajuato, and the people of the country came flocking to his aid, bringing his army to twenty-five thousand strong. The Spanish garrison at Guanajuato was defeated and the city captured. After successful battles at Morelia and Valladolid, Father Hidalgo marched toward Mexico City, but when almost within sight of the capital he was defeated, driven back, and his army dispersed. Father Hidalgo and his officers were betrayed and captured. He was executed at Chihuahua, the thirty-first of July, 1811. And now, Luis, as you see, the big celebrations which we hold every sixteenth of September are in honor of the man who started the struggle for Mexican Independence—a struggle which lasted eleven years. During that time Mexican soil was stained with blood, but that blood spilled on the battlefield was not shed in vain!" concluded Don Pablo.

"That is a beautiful story, sir. I wish I were a great man like Father Hidalgo," I said, as Don Pablo's wife went to the kitchen and brought a pot of hot coffee.

That night when I went to bed I intended to get up early the next morning and go out to face the world. When I went to bed I felt very comfortable and full of ambition, but the next morning when I awoke, I had such an awful chill and sore throat that I decided to stay in bed all that day. The following morning my throat was worse, and my body ached all over. Immediately a doctor was summoned. He questioned me and found that the mosquito bites, the clear running water which I had drunk, and the fruits I had eaten on my trip had been the cause of my getting a severe case of tropical malaria.

Six weeks of constant home treatments cured my tropical malaria, and I was well enough to go away from Cananea, but I had no money; so the only thing that was left for me to do was to get out and look for a job.

One morning while I was looking for work close to the parade grounds, I passed two well-dressed army officers, who turned and addressed me by my first name. One of them shouted at me, "Luis! Luis! Halt there!"

The other officer came and stood in front of me, pointing his finger at my face, saying, *"Coyote!"*

"Yes, sirs," I answered.

"We have orders to arrest you," said one.

"Why?" I asked.

"Because you have failed to report to your battalion," shouted the first one to me.

"You are a deserter. You are a criminal! You have violated Article 13, Section C of the Rebel Constitution," said the second officer.

After taking a small book from his coat pocket, the first man spoke to me again in a very stern voice. "Yes, *Coyote*, Article 13, Section C of the Rebel Constitution reads—let me see—" he grumbled, while clumsily turning the pages of his book of rules and regulations.

"Ah—here it is." Again he started, "Article 13, Section C of the Rebel Constitution states: 'Any commissioned or noncommissioned officer, soldier, or civilian who is connected in any form with the Contreras Rebel Army; if by his unconquerable efforts, while in the line of duty, or off the battlefield, performs an act, or fulfills a deed of bravery, shall be rewarded with medals in due—'"

"No—Captain—no! You are reading the wrong article!" interrupted the other officer. "You are reading Article 13, Section B, which rewards heroes. *El Coyote* is no hero—he is a deserter, a fugitive, a criminal!"

"Hell! I made an error," said the captain, turning and smiling at the officer who corrected him. Then he turned back to me and started again to speak dramatically, "Article 13, Section C of the Rebel Constitution reads: 'Any commissioned or noncommissioned officer, soldier or otherwise, who is connected in any way with the Contreras Rebel Army, who deserts while engaged in battle shall be shot at sunrise!'"

"Yes, *Coyote*—'shall be shot at sunrise,'" affirmed the other officer.

"But, I—I—I am not a deserter, nor a criminal," I stammered.

"Yes, you are!" one of them shouted, while the other took his pistol from the holster, and poking my ribs with the muzzle of it, commanded me to march ahead of them toward the local jail.

My first night in the Cananea jail was one of the most horrible nights that I had ever gone through. I was confined in solitude by order of my two captors, who, with a very ornamental scrawl, wrote on the county jail's gigantic ledger the following inscription: "*We,* the duly appointed officers of the Contreras Rebel Army, state in this civil document that *we* have apprehended a man—rather a boy—otherwise known to his battalion and his comrades as Luis Pérez, alias *El Coyote.* He is a deserter! a fugitive! a criminal! He should be guarded by a special sentry day and night, and he should be punished according to Article 13, Section C of the Rebel Constitution. Written and signed by Captains Pedro Romero and Tomás Techos." This statement was read to me the next morning by a court judge.

The day I was taken to jail, after a few court formalities at the sergeant's desk, the jailer took me by the arm and pulled me to my cell. As he was leading me, he asked, "Son, what else did you do, besides deserting the rebels?"

"That is all, jailer."

"Why do they say that you are a criminal?"

"I do not know, sir."

"Are you sure you have not been making love to the general's daughters?"

"Oh, no! I do not make love *yet*. I am still too young to make love."

"Hmm-m-m, the young ones are the most dangerous," he murmured. "Just the other day, some officers brought in three fellows who were fooling around with the general's wife and daughters. One of them is doomed to be shot at sunrise tomorrow morning." Then the jailer, after looking around, placed his thick, greasy finger up to his lips, and said, "Sh-h-h-sh! The general caught the criminal climbing up to the window with a guitar on his back. The prisoner claims that he was going to sing *La Golondrina* to Doña Manuela."

"And who is Doña Manuela, *señor* jailer?"

"Why, *muchacho*, Doña Manuela is the general's wife. Didn't you know?"

"No, sir, I did not."

"Yes, and she is a beauty. Just the other day—well—about three months ago, while I was on my way to see a lady friend of mine and my sister Maria, I saw Doña Manuela out in the yard playing with the dogs. And what do you think?" Again putting his soiled finger up to his lips, he said, "Sh-h-h-sh!" Finally he came closer to me and whispered in my ear. "She was barelegged that day! And, young fellow, she surely has the most beautiful legs you ever expect to see on any female! They are perfect!"

"Where was the—"

Suddenly he seemed to remember something and hurriedly interrupted me, saying, "Well, son, for you I feel sorry, but duty is duty and I must obey. This is going to be your new home until the commander will send you to the gallows." Then pointing to the cell in which he was ordered to lock me, he continued, "This is a good calaboose. We have had several prominent criminals in here. We had one fellow here for three weeks, but he was decapitated this morning. Before he died he told me that he had a trained mouse in this cell. He told me that the mouse's name was Pepino. Have you ever heard of a little rat being named Cucumber?"

"No, sir, I haven't," I answered.

"Don't kill him if you see him running up and down the dungeon."

"No, *señor* jailer, I shall not kill Pepino," I said, as the jailer locked the cell and left me there alone.

The cell in which I was confined was a smelly one. The only light available was a dim ray that penetrated through the foot-square peephole, which was reinforced with cross bars. The guards walked continuously, and silently, from end to end of the building until ten o'clock at night, when they began to shout a military password. The cry continued every half hour from the time the lights were put out until sunrise.

Once the special sentinel who was guarding me passed by my cell and loudly shouted, "Twelve o'clock—and all is well here!" The other guards answered the call in a similar manner, to let each other know that they were on duty.

At a later hour the same guard went by my cell, and again shouted the password. Then I walked to the peephole and exclaimed, "Yes, sentinel! Everything might be well there with you, but *nothing* is right here with me."

"What is the matter with you, *muchacho*? Are you not happy in your new home?" he asked, resting the muzzle of his carbine in the peephole.

"Of course not! How do you expect me to be happy when—"

"And why are you not happy, may I ask?" he abruptly interrupted.

Immediately I answered, "I am not happy here because I am cold, hungry, and sleepy."

"Why don't you go to bed?"

"Because there is no bed here, and the floor of this room is wet and cold. Moreover, the bedbugs are eating me alive."

"Ha-ha-ha!" Loudly he laughed; then he said, "Bedbugs in that room and there is not even a *bed* in the place—he-he-he!"

"Well, whether they are bedbugs or other vermin, they are eating me alive."

Changing his manner to one more serious, he said, "Don't worry about the bedbugs, boy; you probably will be shot at sunrise."

"Shot at sunrise!" I exclaimed.

"Yes, shot at sunrise! You are a war deserter, and the army has no use for deserters." Then, shouldering his rifle, he resumed his pacing from one end of the building to the other.

After I heard that I was going to be executed at sunrise, I could not be quite sure whether I was trembling because I was cold, or because I was frightened almost to death. I felt worse that moment than I did the night when my Mauser kicked me over, while I was fighting the last Mexican Federal Troops in Guaymas.

As soon as I was able to realize that things were worse than I had thought, I went away from where I was standing to a corner of the dingy room, and knelt to pray. I parroted my repertoire of prayers to my collection of saints, even though I did not have much faith in them, asking them to forgive my faults, to guide me and to give me courage and strength to face the firing squad in the morning.

The time seemed to drag, but while I was still invoking the host of heaven to come to my rescue, I heard the faint beating of a muffled drum, marking time to an eight-man squad which was approaching the main gate. Immediately I left my place of prayer and went to look out through the barred peephole.

The squad was commanded by a young lieutenant, and as the marching men slowly arrived at the entrance the commanding officer shouted, "Squad—halt! Order—arms!"

After these maneuvers were clumsily performed, the young officer, with sword in hand, saluted the guard and asked him for the prisoner. The overzealous sentry instead of answering the commander's question, shouted "Corporal of the guard! Corporal of the guard!" Then he continued his pacing.

The corporal of the guard came running, rubbing his eyes and making a salute at the same time. Then he said, "On duty my General—I mean—my Lieutenant."

Again the commanding officer raised his shiny sword to the level of his cap visor, saluted the corporal, and asked for the prisoner.

"Ah—the prisoner!" smilingly exclaimed the corporal.

"Yes, the prisoner," repeated the lieutenant.

"Yes, *Commandante*. If you march your men this way, I will deliver the culprit to you," said the corporal.

The officer then shouted, "Squad—attention! Right—face! Forward—march!"

Seven of the men turned to the right and one to the left, then marched. Immediately the lieutenant halted the squad and said, "Pancho, you stupid ass! Don't you know your right from your left? Instead of the prisoner, you should be the man to be shot today!"

At this comment Pancho turned to the right and joined his comrades, who were laughing at him, and the squad was ordered to follow the corporal. The corporal and the officer were at the head of the squad, and when they came close to the door of my cell the corporal said, "*Señor* lieutenant, the prisoner is in cell number three."

Heretofore I had thought that I was the only prisoner in the Cananea jail, and when I heard the corporal tell the commanding officer that the man who was going to be shot that morning was in cell number three, I tried to see if three was the number on my cell door.

The corporal went past my cell to door number three, and holding a bunch of keys, he said, "This is the place, *Señor Commandante.*"

The officer commanded the squad to halt. Then the corporal went and opened the door next to mine. As he opened it he exclaimed, "My God! The prisoner has hanged himself!"

As I heard the corporal's exclamation my legs gave way, and I fell into a dead faint.

16

I do not know how long I was unconscious, but upon recovering I found myself in the guard's quarters, surrounded by several curious soldiers.

As soon as I opened my eyes, the sergeant in charge said to me, *"Muchacho,* we are not going to kill you yet—we haven't any orders to do so; but we have orders to keep you in jail until further notice. You may stay here with us until ten o'clock, when your case is to be tried."

"Thank you, Sergeant," I replied. Then I took a gold ring which I had in my watch pocket and handed it to him.

"Why are you giving me this ring?" he asked. "I cannot save you from the firing squad."

"I know that, Sergeant. I know that you are not able to save me from the firing squad, but you have given me news that you are not shooting me this morning. Your news may not save my life, but at least it has saved my nerves."

At this remark one of the soldiers near us turned to another and said, *"Carambas,* the boy has brains!"

"Muchacho," said the sergeant, "you better keep your ring. Wear it yourself."

"No, Sergeant," I replied, "it is a token of friendship from me to you—besides, I have no use for the ring any more. I have lost my ring finger, and I cannot wear it on any other."

Reluctantly he took the ring and put it on his little finger; then he gave me a cup of coffee and said, "My boy, I will do all that I possibly can to help you, and promise that I will feed you as long as you remain in this jail."

I thanked the sergeant for his kindness, and as I was doing so, one of the rebels shouted, "Long live the sergeant! Long live the boy! *Vivan todos los hombres valientes!"*

"Long live Mexico! And long live all the brave men," repeated another soldier, as an answer to the cheers.

It was a joyful moment for the sergeant, and as soon as he heard the first shout, he held his chest up high and saluted the men present.

At ten o'clock I was taken to a court room, and when the judge arrived, he asked, "Where is the prisoner?"

The bailiff took me by the arm and said, "Your Honor, here he is." Then the bailiff took me closer to the judge's bench and continued, "This is the prisoner, Your Honor."

At this the judge looked at me and said, "Good morning, young man." Then he paused for a while to fix his glasses on his nose, and picked up the civil document. After he had opened the ledger he said, "Here we are." Then he read: "'*We,* the duly appointed officers of the Contreras Rebel Army, state in this civil document that *we* have apprehended a man—rather a boy—otherwise known to his battalion and comrades as Luis Pérez, alias *El Coyote.* He is a deserter! a fugitive! a criminal! He should be guarded by a special sentry day and night, and he should be punished according to Article 13, Section C of the Rebel Constitution. Written and signed by Captains Pedro Ramos and Tomás Techos.' Hmmmm-m, Article 13, Section C of the Rebel Constitution—" he mumbled between his teeth. Then he stood, and in a very majestic tone addressed the listeners: "Gentlemen, this Civil Court has no jurisdiction whatsoever to enter verdict against a war deserter. However, this Court has the right to sentence an army prisoner to jail until he, or the party in question, is tried or set free by orders of a court-martial. Therefore, I, the appointed judge of this Civil Court of the town of Cananea, sentence this prisoner of war—" pointing to me, "known to his battalion and his comrades as Luis Pérez, alias *El Coyote*, to serve time in jail until further notice. The court is now adjourned.'"

Immediately I was taken back to my cell by the jailer, and when he was opening the door he asked, "Did you sleep well last night?"

"No, *señor*, I did not sleep at all."

"Didn't you? Did you see Pepino?"

"No, *señor*, but I heard him."

"You heard Pepino, boy? He is just a baby rat."

"Yes, but just the same, I heard him gnawing something."

"Maybe he was hungry, do you think, eh? I am going to bring some old tortillas for him to eat." Then, closing the cell door, he left.

A few minutes later the jailer came back to the cell bringing two blankets, a crate, and a plate of beans with three corn tortillas. After he opened the gate he said, "Little man, I brought you something to eat, and these blankets for you to sleep on."

I took the food and the blankets, and after I had thanked him, he put down the crate and said, "Little one, I like you. My name is Pancho Moreno de Leon, but you can call me Pancho."

While I was eating my beans, there came trailing into the cell the most forlorn mastiff I had ever seen. He looked more like a consumptive mountain lion than a watchdog. When the jailer saw him, he said to me, "This dog is our pet."

"Is he a high-class dog?" I asked.

"*Carambas*, no—he is a mixture. He is crossed between a Saint Bernard and a Mexican coyote. The commandante brought him here when he was still a baby pup. He calls him Fatima, on account of the Egyptian wiggle he displays when he trots."

As I was eating the beans, the dog sniffed my back; then the jail-keeper said, "Fatima likes you too. And I think he feels sorry for you."

"I like him, too," I replied, feeding the dog a piece of tortilla with beans. Then I asked, "*Señor*, how long have you been a jailer?"

"Well, let me see, boy," mumbled Pancho to himself. "Pedro, my son, was three years old, and my sister Maria was going to have a baby." Then speaking to me directly he said, "Now I remember. Twelve years, to be exact."

"That is a long time," I remarked.

"Yes, my little one, and in twelve years I have lost only three prisoners." Then coming closer to me he whispered, "I lost them because I let them escape. They were not real criminals nor army deserters like you. They were only *loco* about women."

"Were they?"

"Yes, that is why I left the gate open."

"Didn't you get punished for letting them go?"

"No, my boy, the *commandante* never missed them." Then he arose, and while he was locking the cell door he said, "I'll come and see you tonight."

About seven o'clock he came back again, followed by Fatima. This time he brought me more beans and tortillas, and he also brought a bottle of tequila. After he had handed me the plate with the food, he said, "I never like to drink alone. Do you want a drink?"

"No, sir, I don't drink, thank you."

He sat on the crate, and as he was putting the bottle on the floor, he looked toward one of the corners of the cell and exclaimed, "Look! I see Pepino."

"Where?"

"There in his hole," he replied, walking toward the corner. When he was near the place he squatted, and taking a hard tortilla from his shirt bosom, he called, "Here, Pepino, here, don't be afraid. For you I brought a tortilla for your supper." After leaving the Mexican pancake near Pepino's hole, he came back to the crate and said, "Watch, he'll come out."

A few moments later the mouse came and sniffed the tortilla, then ran back. Again he ran back, but immediately turned and came toward the dog, who was sleeping close to me. As the mouse was sniffing near the mastiff, I said to the jailer, "You had better chase Pepino back to his hole because the dog will kill him."

"No, Fatima won't kill a fly," replied the jailkeeper, picking up the bottle and taking a drink. While the man was drinking, Fatima opened one eye, and almost like an automatic monster, he raised his massive paw and flattened Pepino to a pulp. At Pepino's squeaks the jailer dropped the bottle and swore, *"Perro cabrón!* You killed Pepino!" Then he picked up the dying mouse by the tail and went out of the dungeon shouting, "Fatima killed Pepino! Fatima will pay for this!"

While Pancho, the jailer, was away from the cell Fatima got up, scratched off a few fleas, then wobbled over to the rat hole, brought the hard tortilla to my bedding, and ate it. Soon the jailkeeper came back, without the mouse, and said, "Pepino is dead and I am going to punish that damned dog for killing my—"

"What are you going to do to him?" I interrupted.

"I'm going to lock him in here with you. He is a murderer and you are an army deserter." Then he locked the dog and me in the smelly calaboose.

The following morning the jailer came in very early. The dog was restless, and as soon as the cell door was opened he bolted out, almost knocking down the jailkeeper. As the dog whizzed out the door, Pancho shouted, *"Perro cabrón!* He is no good for nothing. As soon as I will get hold of him I am going to give him five lashes for killing my Pepino." Then speaking directly to me he said, "Boy, I have good news for you."

"You have? Am I free?" I asked.

"No, but the sergeant pleaded for you, and he is going to be responsible for you until you are tried by a court-martial. However, you have to stay in the guard's quarters."

"Oh, I don't mind that," I said, as he helped me to gather my blankets and took me to the guard's quarters. There the sergeant and I became good friends, and whenever he was on duty, he would let me go out to a show, or to visit some of my acquaintances.

As no one came to claim me I had to remain in jail fourteen days. While there I became very friendly with the guards, and felt quite at home. It was not so bad to be in jail in Mexico because there were always a lot of interesting things that happened to the prisoners. Each man in jail was on his own honor, and after proving that he was a worthy person, he was allowed to go out at will on the condition that he would report every day until his term expired.

On Saturdays, Sundays, and holidays there was always a social reunion in the patio of the jail. The families of the prisoners came and brought tortillas, tamales, coffee, enchiladas, and beans. The guests and the prisoners played their musical instruments, sang, drank, and danced. At the end of each jail fiesta, the prisoners and their friends sang to the accompaniment of a guitar a verse known as *El Epitafio de la vida* (The Epitaph of Life).

"Let the world slide, let the world go;
A fig for care, a fig for woe;
If I can't pay, why I can owe,
And death makes equal the high and low."

At the close of the epitaph a great "Long live Mexico!" resounded through the halls; then the visitors went home and the prisoners were ordered to their cells.

One morning, while I was playing stud poker with the off-duty guards, the jailer received orders to get ready to move, and to take all the prisoners along because the Moralistas were coming to attack the town of Cananea.

While the stationed army and the prisoners were getting ready, my friend the sergeant came to me and said, *"Coyotito*, you better take this Mauser and come with us."

I took the rifle and thanked him for it. To my thanks he replied, *"Coyote*, you are in the army again. You are a free man—a free soldier—a free fighter! Think of it!" And holding the bayonet of his Mauser over my right shoulder, he said, "I, the sergeant on duty at the Cananea jail, hereby re-enlist *you* in the Contreras Rebel Army to fight the outlaws!" Then performing a military salute, he added, "However, don't shoot until you see the point of their noses," and finished with a wink.

"Yes, Sergeant, I am in the army again," I parroted. "I am a free *muchacho*—I mean a free man. I am a free soldier—and a free fighter!" Then I started polishing my Mauser so as to have it clean and ready to fight the outlaws, as the sergeant had called *our own countrymen!*

Well, whether it was a case of fighting the outlaws, or my own countrymen, the thing that mattered most to me when I was polishing my rifle was that I was not going to be shot at sunrise, and that my suspense was over. In a very short while I was with the rebel army in the Cananea depot, impatiently waiting for the train to take us to Naco, Sonora, where we were going to entrench ourselves to fight the Moralistas.

17

My trip to Naco proved to be a very pleasant one, and the only exciting event that I experienced turned out to be more or less unusual. It happened that while we were traveling to Naco inside of a railroad boxcar, I wanted to go to sleep, and I could not do so because I had in my pockets five silver pesos which I had won from the guards playing poker. My wish was to find a safe place to hide my money so as to keep my comrades from stealing it. Finally, I conceived the idea of putting my five pesos in one of the upper pockets of my khaki blouse and sewing the opening with several rounds of heavy thread. This I managed with some difficulty; then I strung my Mauser over my shoulder and went to sleep. I slept soundly—in fact, so deeply that the next morning when I looked for my money, I was unable to find it. Some clever thief had taken a sharp knife and cut clear around the seam of the pocket, taking with him my carefully hidden pesos and the scrap of khaki, leaving a hole in my blouse next to my heart.

In Naco, the first orders we received from General Contreras were to dig trenches around the town so as to defend it from the Moralistas. Within two weeks after we had taken possession, the Morales party was attacking us, but we were very successful in holding our fortifications.

We were shut in from all communication, and the only way we were able to get food and help was through Naco, Arizona—on the United States border line.

The fight went on from days into weeks, and from weeks into months, and quite often while we were fighting, the general himself would come through the trenches passing cups of tequila. Handing the drinks to the soldiers he would say, *"Muchacho,* if we win this battle, we will be the rulers of the State of Sonora."

After some of these encouraging words, a soldier would feel very patriotic, and shout, "Long live General Contreras!"

Another would answer, *"Viva el libertador del Estado de Sonora!"*

Still others, after hearing the "Long live the liberator of the State of Sonora," would shout "Long live Mexico! Long live the Revolution!" and other cheers.

Our rations, while we were in the trenches, consisted of soda crackers, coffee, canned beans, sardines, and corned beef. Occasionally some daring women would come through the trenches, bringing pots of hot tripe and hominy soup to us.

All through the cold nights could be heard the rifle and machine gun bullets as they whizzed over our heads. Quite often cannon shells would explode close to us, but we would only bury ourselves deeper in our trenches.

One night the general came through the trenches asking for volunteers to go out to plant a dynamite mine under a railroad bridge about a mile away from our dugouts. The sergeant to whom I had given my gold ring when I was in the Cananea jail came to me and said, *"Coyote,* I want you to come along with us to set the mine. You will carry the fuses, your rifle and this American-made flashlight."

"Sergeant, I do not think that I should go with you," I said.

"It is not what you think—I am your sergeant, and I am commanding you to come with us!"

"Who is us, may I ask?"

"Captain Torrés, Glass-eye, nine other men, you, and myself."

"All right, I'll go. Where are the fuses and the American flashlight?"

"Here, here they are." Smiling, he handed me the flashlight, a small box of fuses, and a roll of fine copper wire.

The captain came closer to the soldiers and asked, "Boys, are you ready?"

"Yes, my Captain, we are ready," answered the sergeant.

Then the captain called José, the man who was nicknamed Glass-eye, and said, "José, you take the battery; you understand more about that diabolic thing than I do."

"Yes, my Captain, yes. I understand the works of the American battery," said José.

This time the captain called the other nine men and said, "Men, each of you take a box of dynamite, and be very careful with it because—well—because dynamite is very dangerous."

"We will be very careful," mumbled one of the volunteers.

"Sergeant!" shouted the captain.

"Yes, Captain," saluted the sergeant.

"Where are the fuses and the wire?"

"*El Coyote* has the fuses and the wire," was the sergeant's answer.

"Is *El Coyote* going with us?" asked the captain.

"Yes," answered the sergeant, "he is one of the volunteers."

Just then I came out of my trench wrapped in my blanket, with my rifle strapped over my shoulder. I was also carrying in my hands the box of fuses, the flashlight, and the roll of fine copper wire. When I heard the sergeant tell the captain that I was a volunteer, bravely I said to the commander, "Yes, my Captain, I am one of the volunteers."

"Good, *Coyote*, good—we need men like you," answered the captain. Then he turned to the group of volunteers and asked, "Are you ready?"

We all answered with one great "Yes, my Captain, we are ready!"

The captain then said, "Sergeant, I will lead the way; then you will send the men with the dynamite, one by one. After you have sent all of them, you and *El Coyote* will follow us." Then to us all he said, "Don't fail me, boys. I am depending on you."

Immediately the sergeant said, "I am at your orders, my Captain, and you can depend on me." We also assured the leader that we were with him.

When the captain was ready, with gun in hand, he called José, and said, "Glass-eye, you come along with me!"

Then—the march began.

18

Captain Torres and Glass-eye led the march, followed by the dynamite men in single file; then came the sergeant and I. While we were walking westward along the south side of the high railroad bank, the rifle and the machine-gun bullets whizzed over our heads. Several times we had to squat to keep from getting hit.

At the end of an hour, all of us were under the railroad bridge setting the mine. We packed the dynamite cases under the steel beams of the trestle, and each case had within it a stick of dynamite with a fuse embedded at one end. The fuses, in turn, were attached to the ends of copper wires, which were attached to the battery. The battery was then placed underneath one of the rails in such a manner that any weight or disturbance might set the electric current in action.

After everything was ready, the captain and Glass-eye started the march back to our trenches. We followed in about the same manner as we had when we went to set the mine. On our way back the rifle and artillery firing from the opposite party was heavier than before. The cannon shells roared through the air, leaving behind them temporary flashes of light.

When the sergeant and I were about half a city block from our fortifications, the sergeant suddenly uttered an awful groan. I came closer to him and asked, "What is the matter, Sergeant?"

"The sons of Satan got me, *Coyote*. Run for your life, run—ooooh—my side. Run, *Coyote*, run! Ooooh—my side!"

"I cannot leave you here, my friend," I said.

"Yes; *Coyote*, you better get away from here! Go—*los cabrones* are coming closer and closer—go—oooh—my side!"

After this scream of pain, he extended his hand and said, "Here, little friend, take this; it is yours," handing me the gold ring which I had given him when I was in the Cananea jail.

I took the ring. Then I tried to straddle the sergeant over my back, but he was too heavy for me, and so I carefully let him down again, and grabbed my rifle, saying, "Sergeant, I am going to get help to take you in."

"No, no, *Coyote*—it is no use—the sons of *las bichas* got me. You run and get away from the bullets. Leave me here to die—I am dying for my country—*Viva México!*"

"Never, Sergeant, never! As long as I am still alive, I shall go and get help to bring you back to our camp." Then I ran toward the trenches.

While I was running a cannon shell whizzed over my head. Immediately I threw myself face down on the ground, and just then the shell burst against the high railroad bank. When I heard the explosion I had visions of having been blown to pieces, but in a few seconds I discovered that I was still all in one piece. Then I picked up my Mauser and ran.

When Captain Torres heard the sound of my hurrying feet, he called, "Sergeant, are you safe?"

"No, the sergeant is wounded. I came to get help to bring him in," I said.

"Wounded?"

"Yes, we must go and get him."

"We cannot go now; the firing is too heavy," he replied.

"Hell with the firing! We have to get the sergeant back. He was good enough to help you to set the mine. Now we have to go and get him."

By this time I had cocked my Mauser, and I was ready to shoot at the captain for his heartlessness. When he saw that I was determined to do something, he said, "All right, *Coyote cabrón,* we shall go." Then turning to one of the dugouts, he called Glass-eye to help us.

The three of us brought the sergeant back to the Red Cross for treatment. He had bled so much that he was weak and unable to talk, but I think he knew that his friends were still with him.

While the doctor was cleaning the sergeant's wound, we heard a very terrific double explosion that came from the direction of our dynamite mine. At the sound of it, the captain said, "There she goes!"

At the same time the doctor turned to us and said, "Yes—and *he* is also gone!" Then he turned back and covered the sergeant's face with the end of my blanket in which I had wrapped him.

As we heard the doctor's statement we bowed our heads. Then, after making the sign of the cross, we filed out one by one and sadly went back to our trenches.

Later in the morning we learned that the enemy had started a loco-motive pushing a boxcar loaded with cases of dynamite set to explode as it would strike our trenches. As it happened, when the weight of the train pressed against the battery of our mine, the dynamite under the bridge exploded, causing the stuff that was on the boxcar also to explode.

The death of my friend, the sergeant, and the double explosion shattered my nerves, and caused me to decide to desert the rebel army for ever.

Early one cold morning, while the Contreras and Morales Rebel Armies were blindly shooting at each other, I was near the American border at Naco, nervously watching and waiting for the immigration patrolman to turn his back, and thus give me a chance to sneak into the United States.

19

After the patrolman had gone by, I rolled under a barbed wire fence into the United States. Once over the line I felt safe, but lay flat on my belly for a few minutes to make sure that the patrolman was out of sight. As soon as I saw my way clear, I started up the road that led to Bisbee, Arizona, and after three or four hours of walking, hiding, crawling, and running, I found myself on top of a high hill. From that location I was able to see the clean-looking town of Bisbee on one side, and on the other, the mournful Naco's battlegrounds. While I was mentally reviewing my exciting past and pondering about my future, I felt so tired and miserable that I sat down under a green shrub and fell asleep.

The barking of a number of dogs, the noise of a cow bell attached to a sheep's neck, and the shouts of an old shepherd woke me from my restful slumber. I could tell by the sun that it was about five o'clock in the afternoon.

As soon as I realized that I was hungry and cold, I decided to go down to a small dilapidated shack which stood a short distance from me. When I reached the place and was trying to break in, I heard shouts from somewhere that sounded to me something like, "Hey, yu! Huat da hell ar' yu dooin' dere?"

When I saw the person who had shouted at me, I stopped trying to get into the house and waited, trembling with fear as well as with cold, until he came closer. When he arrived I heard him say something else that sounded even more complicated. At the completion of his speech, I said, *"Yo no comprendo el inglés."*

Then he waved his hands up and down and said something that sounded to me like, "Me no sabay."

To that I said imploringly, *"Señor, yo tengo mucho hambre y sed. Yo estoy muy cansado y quiero dormir."*

When I had finished saying, "Sir, I am very hungry and thirsty. I am very tired and I want to sleep," he held his arms up again, saying, "Vamoos! Vamoos!"

"Oh, no, mee no vamoos; mee *hambre—sabe hambre?*" And I rubbed my stomach.

"Ah! Hungry eh?"

"Si, mee hoongree."

Then he went into the shack, and in a few minutes came out bringing a plate heaped with cold baked pork and beans, a glass of water, and half a loaf of homemade bread.

While I was eating the food, a boy about twenty years old appeared from somewhere, carrying several books under his arm. The boy and the man talked about something for a few minutes; then the boy came close to me and tried to speak Spanish, asking, "*Co-co—mo se lla—ma u—usted?*"

After I had answered, giving him my name, he went back and talked to the man for some time. Again the boy came back and asked me, "*De dón—de vie—ne usted, y par—par—y—para—*"

Here he stopped and went inside the house. Returning with a large book, he opened it in about the center then started his Spanish conversation again, "*De dónde viene usted, y para dónde va?*" Then he repeated the same thing in English: "Where are you coming from and where are you going?"

When I told him that I had come from Naco and that I was on my way to Douglas, he and the man brought a roll of maps out of the house and tried to explain to me the shortest route to my destination.

Finally the sun went down, and the man told the boy to ask me to spend the night with them. I did stay with them, and that night I rested quite well.

Early the following morning the man was very busy, making coffee, frying ham and eggs, and making biscuits. About six-thirty he called the boy and me to breakfast.

As we sat down at the table, they closed their eyes; then the man murmured something which I thought might have been a prayer. While they had their eyes closed, I reached and took a hot biscuit and put it in my pocket. I just had time to put my hands back in my lap when the man opened his eyes and told the boy something, which in turn the young chap related to me in Spanish.

In a very courteous and kind manner the young man said to me, "My father wishes you to do him the favor of closing your eyes while he thanks God for His kindness and bountiful blessings."

Thanking God at the table just before eating was a new thing to me, and so at the request I closed one eye tight and kept the other half open to see what was going to happen. The man then continued his prayer, and as soon as he said "Amen" I opened my eyes. Then I saw the father of the boy putting three biscuits on his plate, and three on the boy's plate, leaving only two on the biscuit pan. After he saw that there were only two biscuits left in the pan he was holding, he looked at the boy, then at me. Again he looked at the boy and said something to him, holding three fingers in the air, perhaps meaning that he had made three biscuits for each of us. Finally he gave me two biscuits, then took one from his son's plate and divided it between the two of us.

When breakfast was over, the father told his son to tell me to take the old blanket which they had loaned me the night before. They also gave me a small paper bag filled with sandwiches, and the boy, while on his way to the school, put me on the right road toward Douglas.

20

Once on my way to Douglas on foot, I took my time. Quite often I was frightened by the unusual sounds of birds and the noises of strange animals. Somewhere around noon I sat under a railroad bridge and ate half of my lunch. While I was enjoying my sandwiches, I suddenly remembered the biscuit I had stolen early that day. I felt quite bad about having taken the biscuit; and I felt worse after I had taken it out of my pocket, because it was all crumbled to bits. That morning, after the man had asked his son to tell me I could take the blanket, and when he himself had handed me the paper bag with the food, I felt so ashamed that I wanted to vindicate myself by confessing I had taken the biscuit from the table while he was thanking the Lord. But since I was unable to speak English, I thought it would be better to remain silent and go to hell to pay for the unforgivable crime of stealing a biscuit.

At sundown I was very close to the large Douglas ore smelters, and while I was contemplating the panoramic view of my new surroundings, I decided to spend the night in a narrow culvert under a highway.

In my underground abode I made a very comfortable bed with dry grass and the old blanket. The only thing I found wrong with my temporary dwelling was that early the next morning it started to rain, and the running water drove me out of my tunnel bed.

As I was crawling out of the culvert, pushing my half-soaked blanket before me, I saw a beautiful black and white animal which resembled a cat. It was running ahead of me. Suddenly it stopped, and presenting its bushy tail, it sprayed my blanket and one side of my shoulder with a most obnoxious "perfume," causing me to cast away my blanket and my army blouse.

My rest having been broken by the rain and the sad experience with the American polecat, I began my march toward the city. While I was crossing through the smelter yards in the outskirts of the town, I saw several groups of Mexican and American men with lunch buckets in hand, coming to work. As the small crowds of workers passed me, some of the most impolite ones would wrinkle their noses, and one of them said to another, "Whew! Do you smell the skunk? Ain't it awful?"

"Yes, it is terrible!" I heard someone answer.

Another one asked, with a sly wink at his friend, as he eyed me, "I wonder where the hell the skunk could be?"

"I do not know, but I reckon it is mighty close," answered the fellow.

A young worker, who seemed to be intoxicated, pointed at me and said to his partner, "God should not let the skunks run wild, like that, and spoil the air for us Christians."

"Indeed not. If I had my way I would kill every one of them," replied his pal.

As I was passing the different groups of laborers, I looked closely to see if I could recognize anyone. To my disappointment, I was not able to see a familiar face in the long string of workers; so I kept on walking, bearing their ridicule.

While crossing the city railroad tracks, I saw at a distance a familiar person coming toward me. The closer we came to each other the surer I felt that I had met him before. Upon coming face to face with him, I found that he was my long lost uncle.

As he recognized me, he asked without showing a sign of emotion, "What are you doing here, Luis?"

"Nothing, Uncle," I replied.

"Where are you going?"

"No place, Uncle."

"Well, you better go home. Do you see that place over there across that pile of railroad ties?" He pointed to an old shack that was about four blocks away.

"Yes, Uncle, I see it."

"We live there; your aunt is there alone. Go over right away and have something to eat, but be careful and don't frighten her. She has been sick and she is very nervous—and—" sniffing, "you better take a bath—you stink!"

"Yes, Uncle, I shall," I replied, as I started to walk away from him.

As I was leaving, he said, "I will be back at five, and then we will talk things over."

"Very well, Uncle," I answered, and to the shack I went.

When I knocked, my aunt came and slightly opened a squeaky

door, and when she saw me, she exclaimed, *"Jesús, María y José, y los dulces nombres de todos los santos!"* After she exclaimed, "Jesus, Mary and Joseph, and sweet names of all the saints," she opened the door wide.

My aunt was so glad to see me that she threw her arms around my neck and kissed me but, as she was holding me tight in her arms, she said, "Phew! Something terrible! What is it?" Then pushing me away from her, she continued, "You better take a bath right this minute! I have never smelled anything like this in my whole life!"

"Take a bath before breakfast?" I asked.

"Yes, a bath before breakfast," she parroted. Then she continued, "Here is the soap, a towel, and there is the tub," pointing to one corner of the house. "Use plenty of soap and water because you surely smell strong," she added.

As I was filling the tub with hot water she came to the door and shouted, "Give me those rags that you are wearing, and here are some of your uncle's clothes."

As I gave her my old clothes, she went away mumbling between her teeth, "This boy surely stinks bad!"

A few minutes later she came back and shouted again through the closed door, "Be sure to use plenty of soap and water. Clean yourself well and come to breakfast. Don't forget to wash the tub after you get through. Wipe off the floor and bring the wet towels with you."

"Yes, Aunt, I will," I replied, and kept on taking my first bath in weeks—in fact, the first bath I had taken in months.

After my refreshing bath I went to the kitchen and found that my aunt had the table already set with a very delicious breakfast for me. When I had consumed all the food she had prepared, I retired and slept until five o'clock, when my uncle came home.

21

A five o'clock I was awakened by my uncle's cyclonic arrival. When he closed the squeaky door after him, he let it go with such force that the sound of it made me jump out of my floor bed. The slam was so terrific that I thought it was a cannon shot. When my uncle went into the kitchen, he threw his lunch pail on the table and shouted at my aunt, "Is dinner ready?"

"Not yet, Miguel," answered the nervous woman.

"What have you been doing all the day? I see that the house is still dirty. It hasn't been cleaned for a week."

"Well, I have had more work to do today than any other day—and besides, I am sick. You don't care if I die, do you?" asked my aunt.

"Where is Luis?" growled my uncle, ignoring her question.

"Luis is in the back room sleeping. He was very tired."

"Did he take a bath?"

"Of course he took a bath. Do you suppose I would have let him stay here without bathing—the way he smelled?"

To that my uncle did not answer, but instead he asked, "What did you do with the fifty cents I gave you yesterday? I bet you have already squandered it on cosmetics?"

"I have spent the money, but not on cosmetics. I bought food with it."

"Hell, I want a drink and I haven't a penny!" exclaimed my uncle.

At this juncture I came into the kitchen and said, "Hello, Uncle!"

"Hello," he replied halfheartedly.

"How is business, Uncle?"

"I have no business," was his abrupt answer. Then looking at me closely, he asked, "Who the hell told you that you could wear my hunting suit?"

"My aunt loaned it to me."

"Yes," said my aunt, "I gave it to him—you look like the devil in it anyway. Besides, you don't expect the boy to run around the house

86

in those skunky pants, do you? Even though we are poor, we can at least have a little sense of respectability."

"To hell with respectability. I paid good money for that suit, and I want to keep it in wearable condition. As soon as we have supper I will go to Don Juan and ask him to lend me three dollars to buy Luis a pair of blue overalls, a shirt, and a pair of shoes. Is food ready? I am starving. I wish you would have dinner ready for me as soon as I come home. You always put up the lousiest lunches!"

"Don't talk so much. Wash your hands and come to eat," commanded my aunt.

"My hands are clean. I washed them at noon."

"All right, come to dinner. You make me sick the way you talk."

"If you don't want me to talk the way I do, why the hell don't you mind your own business?" stormed my uncle.

"Luis, bring that red chair that is near the Victrola, and come to dinner," shouted my aunt, disregarding my uncle's muttering.

After eating we went to visit Don Juan, and from there my uncle and I went to the business section of town, where he bought me a pair of shoes and a pair of secondhand overalls. He said that since he was not able to buy me a cheap shirt, he was going to let me wear one of his. After he had made these purchases we went home, and on the way he bought a bottle of gin.

The next morning before leaving, he said to me, "Luis, I expect you to do a little work around the house. You can go along the railroad tracks and pick wood and coal to keep us warm during the winter. Help your aunt with the house work."

"Yes, Uncle, I shall do that," I said.

So my life in my new home began in about the same manner as when we lived in Cananea. Day in and day out I went along the railroad tracks with a gunny sack on my shoulder, picking up wood and chunks of coal.

One time while I was walking along the tracks, I saw a locomotive standing by a high tank getting water. Between the tank tower and the engine I saw several lumps of coal. I sneaked along the side of the engine and started picking them up. While I was at my task, the fireman, who was on top of the tender, lifted the long heavy pipe from the locomotive water tank, and pushed it up to where it belonged. As he swung it, a torrent of water rolled back in the pipe and landed on top of my head. This was the second bath that I had taken since I came to Douglas.

Another time while I was looking for wood, I climbed inside an empty boxcar to see what I could find. After I had searched inside the car, I came and sat in the doorway to jump off. As I did, a nail caught in my secondhand overalls and ripped one leg open, leaving my buttocks exposed to the elements. When I came home I was properly scolded by my uncle and aunt for my carelessness.

My life with my uncle and aunt was fairly mild and pleasant until one day, about three months after I had come from Naco, my aunt wanted to know the reason why I had run away from home when we lived in Cananea.

"Aunt," I said, "I ran away from home because you were cruel and mean to me."

That statement made her so angry that immediately she got up, seized a mattock handle, and came toward me. When I saw her coming I went out of the house and ran as fast as I could. But I heard her say, "I'll kill you for that when you come home."

Since I did not want to run the risk of being killed by my aunt, I decided to cross the Douglas border line to Mexico.

22

Agua Prieta is the Mexican border town across from Douglas, Arizona. The day I crossed the border to Agua Prieta, I saw that there was great excitement about something. Investigating, I found that the rebel army which was entrenched in Naco, protecting the town, had lost the prolonged battle. I also learned that during that day and the day before the disbanded rebels had been coming into Agua Prieta, the only large town which harbored Contreras troops.

At sundown that same day, I came upon a company of soldiers whose faces looked familiar to me. They were in formation; that is, they were in a very informal column. Some of the rebels stood shifting from one foot to the other. Others leaned on their guns carelessly, chatting companionably.

Suddenly an officer appeared from the *cuartel* with a notebook in his hand. He came close to the company and shouted a command, "Company! Attention!"

The soldiers stopped talking, and fell awkwardly into better formation. When they were at attention the officer continued: "Men, this is the first time we have had the opportunity to call the roll in nine months. All of you know that we were entrenched in Naco, fighting the Moralistas, and for that reason we were not able to get together. The calling of the roll today is to find out how many men have survived the battle of Naco. Those who lost their lives there shall never be forgotten! Their names will live forever! They died there fighting for a just cause—for liberty—for independence for their flag! For the protection of their loved ones! And above all—they died in the battlefield fighting for their country!" He paused for a moment, and after wiping the perspiration from his forehead, continued: "We grieve for them and feel a deep sorrow, but we have every reason to be proud of the fact that they lived and died in the best tradition of the much-criticized Mexican Rebel Army. We, who are alive, must redevote ourselves to serve our great nation, and to finish the job which was so nobly begun by those brave men!" As soon as the officer had finished his speech, he bowed his head; then the soldiers and civilians present went into spasms of shouts and cheers.

A comely lass, who had lost her sweetheart in the battle, shouted from a high window, "*Vivan los jóvenes valientes que murieron peliando por el amor!*"

After the aroused patriotism had been so ardently expressed, and after the *señorita* had cried, "Long live the brave young men who died fighting for love," another officer came from somewhere and shouted, "Company! Attention! Answer to your names if present: Alarcón, Ramon."

"Present," shouted a maimed soldier.

"Alarcón, José."

No one answered.

Again the officer called, "Alarcón, José!"

Someone in the line shouted, presenting his rifle, "Sir, José Alarcón was killed. I saw the sonbitches get him—I was by his side."

The officer put a line across the dead man's name and continued calling the roll. Soon he came to the P's calling, "Pacheco, Lu— Lucas."

"Present," answered Pacheco.

"Perea, Manuel R."

"Present," mumbled Manuel R. Perea.

"Perea, Alfonso."

"Here!" shouted a bugler.

"Peresa, Antonia."

"On guard duty," shouted a sergeant.

"Pérez, Luis."

No one answered.

"Pérez, Luis!" again he shouted.

At the second call I gained a little courage and weakly squeaked from behind the crowd, "Present!" As I answered I came closer toward the formed company.

One of the soldiers in the rear rank turned to me and loudly whispered, "*Coyote*! You did not get killed, did you?"

"No, Pedro, I did not get killed. I got out of Naco just in time."

At this statement a sergeant bawled me out, saying, *"Coyote*, what the hell are you doing out of line. Do you think that you own the army? Get in here!"

"Sergeant, I am not in line because I haven't a rifle. I lost everything in trying to get away from the Moralista *cabrones*, and—"

"Shut up!" he interrupted. "We shall give you another Mauser after roll call."

Pedro, the soldier who saw me first, made room for me and whispered, "Get in, *Coyote*, the sergeant ate bull meat for dinner—he is tough!"

I fell in line, and after the company had been dismissed, I was equipped with an army blanket, a complete uniform, a large ration of staples, and a bigger Mauser than the one I had before. So—again, Luis Pérez, alias *El Coyote*, was an enlisted rebel under Contreras, after having twice been a deserter.

23

The activities of the army in Agua Prieta for the first few weeks were dull and monotonous, except on wash day, and at night when stories were told around the campfires.

Once a week, when not on duty, we were ordered to center our daily tasks about a flowing river. Here, men and women bathed together, discarding their clothing as they reached the depths of the running water. Slender, rounded women, bare to the waist, and sturdy soldiers, unclad from head to foot except for a loincloth, beat their wearing apparel upon rocks until cleaned. Then the laundered garments were spread on the sand or on shrubs to dry. Often while the army was performing the weekly wash, herds of cattle were seen on either side crossing the river, causing the water to turn muddy. Other times burros stood patiently while their masters clambered down the steep banks to fill the water jars. And so wash day in the Mexican rebel army was a pleasant one for me because it was full of fun and excitement.

One night while we were seated by the fire in our open field camp, there came a blond Mexican complaining about not being able to please the general. Since blond Mexicans are so rare, this man was known to us as *Piojo Blanco*, meaning white louse. His real name was Policarpio Rosa Mercado Pinchón. When Policarpio sat by the fire he said, "What the hell is the use! No one can ever please our General."

"What is the matter now, *Piojo Blanco*?" asked one of the soldiers.

"Well," replied Policarpio, lighting a cigarette, "I worked hard making a table for the general's office, and he doesn't like it. He says that it is too wide and too long, and that he doesn't like to stretch so much to get his stuff, and that he even has to get up sometimes to reach his papers."

"*Piojo Blanco*, why don't you do what I did once?" asked *Tecolote*, the man who always liked to tell stories.

"What did you do, *Tecolote mentiroso?*"

"Once, when I was living on the farm with my wife, I built a brick oven with the door facing the north. When one of my best friends came to see us, he said, '*Tecolote*, my friend, your oven is very beautiful, but you should have put the door to the south as the north wind is always harder.' When my friend went away I tore down the damned oven and rebuilt it, with the door to the south to please him. About a week later my brother came from Mexico City, and upon seeing the oven he said, '*Tecolote*, my good brother, you are the most stupid ass I have ever seen. The door of that oven should have been toward the east.' So, while my brother was still visiting us, I tore the blamed oven down and rebuilt it, with the door facing the east. After my brother had gone away, my godfather came to bring me a piece of beef, and when he saw my oven he said, 'My godson, if your oven had the door to the west, you would be more successful in toasting your meat and baking bread.' When my godfather left, I tore down the confounded oven and rebuilt it, with the door to the west. By this time I thought I had pleased some of my friends. But about a month later, my papá came to pay us a visit, and when I took him to the patio to see my oven he said, '*Tecolote*, my son, you are the biggest scatterbrain I have had the opportunity to talk to. You should know by experience that the best way to build an oven is to have the door facing the north. That is the first principle of logic,' said my papá."

"What did you do then, *Tecolote*?" I asked.

"*Coyote*, I got so mad that while my papá was still there, I tore down the troublesome oven, went to the village and bought a car wheel and brought it home. After making a strong base for the wheel, I placed it flat on a pivot, and rebuilt the bedamned oven on top of it. Then when my friends, my brother, my godfather, and my father would say, '*Tecolote*, the door of that oven should be in a certain position,' I would get hold of the wheel and with a quick twist of the hand, I would please them all."

"That is a good idea, *Tecolote*. Tomorrow I am going to make a revolving table for our lazy general. I hope I will be able to please him," said *Piojo Blanco,* as he wrapped himself in his *sarape* for the night.

On March 9, 1916, Pancho Villa and his band of men attacked Columbus, New Mexico, killing several American soldiers and citizens and destroying property. The United States was then ready to fight, and on March 17 General Pershing, with twelve thousand troops, was ordered to invade Mexico in pursuit of Villa and to bring him back, dead or alive. The American forces were attacked by Villa while in Mexico, but they suffered only small losses. On May 2, 1916, after a conference between General Obregón, the Mexican minister of war, and General Frederick Funston, the United States commander on the border, it was conditionally agreed, since Villa had not been captured, to withdraw the American expedition. The American troops were withdrawn and we, the Contreras army, received urgent orders from our general to entrench ourselves in the outskirts of Agua Prieta, because Pancho Villa was coming to attack us.

Immediately the stationed army started to dig trenches and underground protection for the citizens of the town. In a very short time the little city was surrounded with several strands of barbed wire, zigzagging from post to post, making a tricky and tangled web which was almost impassable. The American soldiers also dug a deep trench along the inside of the international line to protect themselves while Villa's army was attacking us.

About a month after we had received orders to fortify ourselves, the Villistas swooped down. At the end of three days of constant fighting, Villa's troops gave up the attack and went to destroy the near-by unprotected Mexican towns. As soon as the Villistas left we followed them.

During our campaign against Villa, outside of Agua Prieta, I experienced a series of interesting and exciting events.

The first night that we were out camping, I was chosen by my company commander to go to the General's tent to make coffee, fry beans, and bake tortillas for General Contreras' supper. The general seemed to be well pleased with my culinary arts, but for a slight error I did not get to be his private cook.

After I had returned to my company from my cooking adventure, Captain Mondragón, my commander, asked, "What is the matter, *Coyote*? Aren't you a good cook?"

"I guess not, Captain. I put salt in the general's coffee instead of sugar," I answered.

"Ha-ha-ha! I should like to have seen him when he tasted the salty coffee."

"Yes, Captain, he looked funny when he spit it out, and he got grounds in his mustache."

"Well, *Coyote*, don't worry. You can be my orderly, and when you become of age I will see that you are made a commander of a battalion," he replied, as he started rolling a cigarette.

"Thank you, my Captain. And what does an orderly do for an officer when he is in his service?"

"Well, there are several things that he should do. When in campaign, like we are now, the orderly should carry the officer's campaign bag and his canteen full of water. When stationed in a city, he should shine the officer's boots, and see that his uniforms are always cleaned," he explained.

"Captain, maybe I can be your orderly only while we are in campaign, because I do not like to shine shoes nor keep uniforms clean."

"Do as you like, *Coyote*." Then pointing to a hook on the tent post, he said, "There is my canteen; you go and fill it with fresh water."

Immediately I took his canteen and mine and went down to the running creek. While I was carefully performing the task of filling the canteens with water, a soldier nicknamed *Loro* approached me and exclaimed, "Hello, *Coyote*. What are you doing with two canteens?"

"*Loro*, if you must know, one of these canteens is mine; the other belongs to Captain Mondragón."

"Ha-ha-ha!" laughed *Loro*. "Captain Mondragón has had twenty orderlies in the last three months, and he has promised to make all of them battalion commanders—ha-ha-ha!"

"What is wrong with that?" I asked.

"What is wrong with that?" he parroted.

"Yes, what—"

"Listen, *Coyote*, Captain Mondragón is a rascal," he interrupted me. "The only way he can get an orderly is by promising to make him a commander, and he gets a lot of work out of those who are stupid enough to believe him. Don't be a fool!"

"Is that right, *Loro*?"

"Of course it is right. If you don't believe me, go and ask Pedro about it. He was his orderly once."

As we were talking we saw Pedro climbing down the steep embankment to get water, and before he reached us, *Loro* shouted, "Pedro, *El Coyote* is Captain Mondragón's orderly now. What do you think of it?"

"No-o-o!" mooed Pedro.

"Ye-e-s!" affirmed *Loro*. "And he is going to make him a battalion commander when he becomes of age."

"Ha-ha-ha!" they chuckled.

Having learned of Captain Mondragón's rascalities, I took my two canteens and went to camp. Pedro and *Loro* remained by the creek laughing at me, and as I walked away, they stood at attention performing a military salute. When I passed by them, Pedro said, "Good-by, Battalion Commander!"

"Good-by, Battalion Commander. I hope I will be your orderly when you become a general," added *Loro*.

That made me so angry that as soon as I returned to the captain, I said, "*Capitán* Mondragón, here is your canteen—I don't want to be your orderly. I'm a busy soldier. I have enlisted in the army to fight the enemy, and not to be an orderly." Then I left his tent and went back to my company.

When I was leaving I heard him say, "What the hell is wrong with all these fellows? They don't want to work for their promotions—that is why we don't have enough generals in this army!"

The following morning we received orders to continue our march against Villa. At about ten o'clock we had an open field battle with the Villistas, and in a few hours we were chasing them all over the hills. Both armies lost several men in that encounter. One of our companies captured forty-three cannons, six machine guns, and twenty prisoners.

As I was coming down a hill I saw a Belgian stallion, and a mule with a machine gun on its back hidden among some oak trees. When I noticed that the quadrupeds were standing still, I stopped and cocked my Mauser. Then I proceeded cautiously toward them. When I reached the animals, I saw that no one was around. Carefully looking at the saddle on the horse, I found several small packs of Villa's paper money. At once I knew that the animals belonged to the Villistas; so I strung my Mauser on my shoulder, took my pistol in hand, and went to the near-by bushes to look for the former owner. When I failed to find him,

I came back, mounted the horse, and led the mule to our temporary camp.

On the way to the camp I was an eyewitness to a cold-blooded, machine gun shooting of twenty-five war prisoners. The effect of seeing the lifeless bodies fall to the ground, stacking one against the other, made me realize that one's life should be occupied with something better than ruthlessly fighting and killing innocent or defenseless people. Right then and there I decided to get out of the army and stay out.

When I arrived at camp with my horse and mule, one of the rebels, nicknamed *Lobo*, shouted, "Hey—*Coyote*—where the hell did you get that elephant?"

"What elephant?" I asked.

"The one you are riding."

"*Lobo*, I admit this horse has the strength of an elephant, but I don't see any other comparison."

"You must be blind, *Coyote*."

"He might look like an elephant to you, but his trunk is not as long as your nose," I replied.

"Ha-ha-ha!" laughed the crowd of rebels, who had gathered around to view my mule and horse.

In a few minutes Captain Mondragón came and shouted, "Break it up, men! Break it up! What the hell is the trouble?"

"*El Coyote* has captured an elephant," cried *Lobo*.

"*Lobo*, how many times must I tell you that my horse is not an elephant."

"Ha-ha-ha!" The crowd roared.

Captain Mondragón commanded, "Attention!" Then turning to me, he said, "*Coyote*, this is the Seventh Battalion of Infantry, and not a cavalry regiment. You better take your beasts to Captain Morales—he will take care of them."

"Yes, *Coyote*, take your elephant to Captain Morales. He will take good care of him for you," shouted *Lobo*.

"*Lobo*, you better mind your own business if you know what is good for you," warned Glass-eye, who had been listening to the conversation.

"Why don't you howl, *Lobo*?" asked one of the rebels.

The crowd laughed uproariously, and I led my animals to Captain

Morales, who took the horse and sent me with the mule to the artillery regiment.

After the two regiments had taken my live stock, I expected to be well compensated for the capture. Several times I thought I would be highly decorated with a medal, and honored with a rank and money, but these never came. So after the disappointment and the horror of having been an eyewitness to the slaughter of helpless young men, I decided to go to General Contreras, and ask him for an honorable discharge from his army.

24

About a week after we had returned to Agua Prieta from the last campaign against Villa, I became an orderly to a newly promoted captain of the Contreras Rebel Army.

One evening about seven-thirty, while I was resting in my commander's tent, he came in, and after a short conversation he said, "*Coyote*, tonight I want you to go with me to La Casa del Amor."

"The House of Love is a brothel, is it not?" I asked.

"Yes, *Coyote*, it is," affirmed the officer.

"Captain, I don't think I should go there with you."

"And why not? A man should know something about everything. You have been a damned good little soldier, and it is high time you should learn something about women. Why, *Coyote*, when I was your age I was an expert at lovemaking. I will never forget the time I was chased by a butcher who caught me with his wife in his own home. That is a fact, *Coyote*."

"Well, Captain, I am your orderly, and I am here to obey orders. I am just like putty, and I can be molded any way to fit the plans of the day."

"Well said, *Coyote*, well said, but I hope that you are not the soft kind of putty. I don't want you to be a jellyfish, and give in without putting up a fight."

"Not me, Captain; I am not a jellyfish."

"That is what I like about my *Coyote*—you are always willing to try everything out, aren't you?"

"Yes, my Captain, I always like to try everything out," I parroted.

Suddenly he asked, "*Coyote*, where in the hell is my blue uniform?"

"It is still in your dressing case, Captain."

"That is the uniform I'm going to wear tonight."

"Yes, Captain."

"Get ready, *Coyote*. I want you to see the girls before they get drunk."

"Yes, my Captain," I continued, while he began to change his clothes.

The officer wore his blue, tailor-made uniform, and I, my dirty army outfit. The only thing I wore worthy of mention was a pair of slightly used handmade guaraches, which I had taken off a dead soldier's feet during the last encounter with Villa.

About seven-thirty the captain and I were walking along the first block of cribs. As we were going by the incense-smelling rooms, I could see scantily dressed women of all descriptions sitting on their beds or in the doorways, smoking and calling in some of the men that went by. Here and there I could see small groups of men drinking, talking, and smoking.

At about the middle of the block of cribs, one of the harlots addressed me, "Hello, sonny, did you come to see mamma?"

"Who, me? I—I—"

"No, sonny did not come to see mamma—he came with papa," interrupted the captain.

"Rats! Who in the hell is talking to you? You meddler—why don't you let the kid have a good time?" retorted the woman.

"Because you are not his kind."

"And who the hell are you to tell me whose kind I should be? Are you going to choose the kid's girls?"

"No, but you are not getting him."

"*Chulo cabrón!* Why don't you mind your own business?" shouted the enraged strumpet as she went into her nook, slamming the flimsy door.

The captain turned to me and said, "Come on, *Coyote*, let us go to the dance hall; these whores are putrid."

I followed my commander to the hall and when we were at the door of it, I saw a large counter facing the entrance. Behind the bar there was a fat woman serving drinks. All around the saloon there were men and women seated on chairs and benches. At the further end of the counter there was a piano and a very thin man was playing it. Most of the people there were either drinking, smoking, or necking. In one of the corners of the room, near where the piano stood, there was a man seated on a crate with his big sombrero over his face, as though he were sleeping. When we stepped into the saloon, the fat woman shouted from behind the counter, "Ernesto! Ernesto!"

The man who I thought was sleeping slowly removed his sombrero from his face and asked, "Yes, *señora*—what do you want?"

"Go and see how old is that boy who came with the gentleman."

Evidently Ernesto was the bouncer. He came to where we were and asked me, "How old are you, *muchacho*?"

"I am—"

"He is old enough to be here," interrupted the captain. "He came with me."

Ernesto did not say anything to us, but turned to the stout woman and shouted, "The *señor capitán* says that the *muchacho* is old enough to be here—he says that he came with him, I think."

When Ernesto had finished shouting he went back to his corner and resumed his position. The bartender only grunted and kept on serving the guests.

After we had been detained by the bouncer, we went to a corner of a bench which was near the counter. As we were sitting down, a painted little *señorita* came and greeted the officer: "Captain Bojorques, how are you? I haven't seen you for a long time. The last time I was with you, you were still a second lieutenant. Where have you been? Who is the little fellow—is he your son?"

"No," replied the captain, "he is my orderly. I brought him here to see the ladies. He is very shy around women. I want him to get used to the girls—you know."

"Yes, I know," murmured the woman; then she asked, "Captain, aren't you going to buy me a drink?"

"Yes, yes, I will," answered the officer, and the three of us went to the counter.

At the bar my commander ordered hard drinks for himself and his companion and for me he ordered an egg punch without liquor. Immediately the corpulent bar maid served the beverages, and while we were drinking, a tall man and a short man got into a fist fight. The big man was getting the better of the little one. Suddenly the small fellow backed away, drew his dagger, and holding it by the point of the blade, threw it at his opponent. The large man ducked, and the wicked steel stuck in the doorframe. When the weapon flew through the air the women screamed, and I ran behind the counter. As I was on my way to hide, somebody fired a shot, and in my excitement I stumbled over some wine bottles and broke several glasses which were on the floor. While I was trying to make myself comfortable under the counter, I felt a large hand grab me by the collar of my khaki blouse. With an unexpected jerk—I was pulled out from my hiding place. It was the heavy-set woman, and when she had me out she grumbled, "Damned boy! You get out of my house and stay out This is not a kindergarten. If I ever see you here again I will kill you!" Then she took me to the door and pushed me onto the board sidewalk.

When I was outside composing myself, I turned and saw on the wall a large lettered sign which stated "Minor generals are also allowed in La Casa del Amor."

After reading it I shouted, "To the devil with The House of Love." Then I continued on my way.

While walking to camp I went by the cribs, and the prostitute who had greeted me when I was with the captain asked, "Well, little one, did you get what you came after? Did the panderer get the right kind of girl for you?"

"Oh, yes, I got more than what I wanted." Then I asked, "How much do you charge?"

"I charge three pesos, but for you—my little one—it will only be two."

"It is not worth that much to me," I answered, continuing my way.

As I was going back to camp I saw a middle-aged woman coming toward me. Apparently she had been drinking, for she swayed from side to side when she walked. As I met her she almost fell off the curb, and I grabbed her arm to keep her from falling. At the same time she embraced me, saying, "My beautiful little man! Where have you been all my—"

"I am not a man yet, *señora*, I am still a boy," I interrupted her.

"That is all right; you have a uniform," she replied, burying my face against her large bosom. As she was pulling me closer to her body, I mumbled, "No, no, *señora*, no!" Then I pulled away, picked up my cap, and ran to camp. As I was running she muttered, "Poor little one, he is not a man; he is just a jellyfish."

About an hour later the captain came back, but I was among the other tents telling the soldiers about my adventures at the bawdyhouse. When I came to the officer's tent he asked, "What happened to you, *Coyote*?"

"Nothing, Captain."

"Nothing!" he repeated, as he started to laugh heartily. Then he added, "You looked so funny in the hands of the madame that I could not help but laugh and let her have a good time with you. You certainly were killing."

"She was killing me!"

"Ha-ha-ha! *Coyote*, you looked like a scared chicken in the claws of a hawk."

"Captain," I said, "La Casa del Amor is not 'The House of Love' for sane people, but a crazy house for persons who have no brains."

"Yes, *Coyote*," he concluded; then in a mocking way he quoted, "'Captain, I am your orderly, and I am here to obey orders. I am just like putty, and I can be molded any way to fit the plans of the day.'" At this he burst out laughing.

When I heard his sneering chuckle I took my blankets, wrapped myself in them, and said to him, "Captain, tomorrow I am resigning my post as an orderly to resume the rank of a common soldier. Good night, *señor Capitán*."

25

Soon after we had returned to our *cuartel* in Agua Prieta, I proceeded, through the regular army routine, to try to get my honorable discharge from the Contreras rebel troops. I tried persistently and, after three failures, I took other measures.

One day during the month of August 1917 at siesta time I walked toward General Contreras' headquarters. As I was approaching the place, the guard on duty shouted, "Halt there! What is your name, rank, and regiment?"

"Private Pérez, Seventh Battalion of Infantry of the Mexican Army; the protectors of the State of Sonora," I replied.

"Corporal of the Guard!" shouted the sentinel. Then turning to me, he added, "Private Pérez, advance to be recognized."

I marched toward him, and the corporal of the guard, who had been disturbed from his siesta, asked, "What can we do for you, Private Pérez?"

"Corporal, I would like to speak to General Contreras."

"State your business to us," said a sergeant who had come from within the building.

"My business is with the general and not with you."

As soon as I had stated that my business was with the general, the corporal seized me and started searching through my clothing. When he had finished, the sergeant asked, "Is he armed?"

"No! He is not armed," replied the corporal in a surprised manner.

"Hold him here until I find out what to do with him," said the sergeant. Then he went into the headquarters, and within five minutes' time he came back and ordered me to follow him. I obeyed, and the corporal came behind me.

As we were going through the wide halls of the building, I saw on one side several fat generals reading the news of the day, playing cards, and chatting. On the other side I saw petty officers gossiping among themselves. When we came to the door of the chamber where General

Contreras was conducting his business, an officer opened the door and, after a military salute, he stated, "General Contreras, Private Pérez, to—"

"Let him in—let him in," interrupted General Contreras.

"Yes, sir," answered the officer, and then commanded me to come in.

When Generalissimo Contreras saw me, he asked, "What can I do for you, young man?" squinting, as he spoke.

To his question I answered, "My General," clicking my heels and putting my right hand up to my forehead, "I wish to obtain an honorable discharge from your army."

"This is very irregular. Why don't you follow the specified form stated in the army Book of Rules and Regulations?" he asked.

"I have, my General."

"When?"

"Three months ago I sent the first one; a month after that I sent the second one, and last month I sent the third application. Since I have not received an answer to any of my three petitions, I decided to come and see you in person."

"And why do you want to leave the army? Don't you like it? Don't we feed you well?"

"Yes, my General. I am quite pleased with the way I am treated in the army, but—"

"But what?" he interrupted.

"My General, I wish to go somewhere—some place where I may be able to go to a school and educate myself."

"Where would you like to go?"

"To the United States, my General."

"Why the United States? Isn't Mexico good enough for you? Mexico is for the Mexican people."

"Oh, yes, my General, but my uncle lives in the United States."

"What part?"

"In Douglas, Arizona, sir."

Changing his form of questioning he continued, "Of which regiment are you a member?"

"I am a member of the Seventh Battalion of Infantry, my General."

"Very well. Wait a few minutes over there," pointing to a chair. Then he rang a bell. An officer appeared and General Contreras ordered him to bring the records of the Seventh Battalion of Infantry.

When the archives were brought to him, the general called me and asked, "You said that your name was Lucas-s-s?"

"No, *señor*, my name is Luis Pérez—otherwise known as *El Coyote.*"

"Oh, yes, Luis Pérez. When and where were you enlisted?"

"I was enlisted in Cananea, but I do not remember the date."

"Hmm-m-m-m," he hummed, then opened one of the books, and with a finger on the page, he mumbled, "K, L, M, N, O, P, P, P, Pérez, Julian, Pérez, Luis— Luis Pérez-z-z—here we are." Then he read: "'Luis Pérez, was enlisted in Cananea in 1914, and deserted the army while fighting in the battle of Rio Verde.'"

Right away I said, "Oh, no, my General. I did not desert the army. I was wounded in the battle of Rio Verde, and I was sent to the hospital in Cananea."

"Hmm-m-m-m, very interesting," he said. Then he asked, "In what part of the body were you wounded?" Immediately I held up my right hand and said, pointing to my third finger, "This is the finger I lost in the battle of Rio Verde."

"How?"

"A wild bullet hit it, I think."

"Hmm-m-m-m, how old are you?"

"I was about eleven when I—"

"When were you born?" he interrupted.

"I was born the twenty-fifth day of August, 1904, in San Luis Potosí."

As I answered, he took a pencil and paper and said, "Well—let me see—1904, and this is 1917. Four from seven, three—zero from one is one—that makes you thirteen years old." Lifting his eyes from the paper he asked, "Do you have a mother and father?"

"No, my General, *soy huérfano.*"

"You are an orphan boy?"

"Yes, sir."

"Well—you have been in the army long enough. I am going to write a note next to this entry of desertion, saying that you are free to go wherever you like."

"Thank you, my General," I said.

After he had finished writing, he stood up, and taking his wallet from his hip pocket, he said, "Here, my young man—take this." He handed me a twenty-dollar bill of United States money. Then he continued, "Buy yourself a suit of civilian clothes. Good-by and God bless you."

I took the money with my left hand, performed a military salute, thanked the general, and went out into the street. Immediately I went to the nearest drygoods store and bought "civvies," including shoes.

From Agua Prieta I went to visit Don Juan, the man who loaned my uncle the three dollars to buy a pair of shoes and overalls for me during my first visit to Douglas.

While I was on my way, I decided that General Contreras was not such a bad *hombre* after all. I considered him a gentleman in many ways, and particularly because he had given me twenty dollars. The only thing that worried me was that I did not become a general of the Mexican army. Later on I thought perhaps the reason was that I had refused to become Captain Mondragón's orderly.

When I arrived at Don Juan's place, he said, "Luis, I have sad news for you."

"What news, Don Juan?"

"Well," he said, bowing his head and making the sign of the cross, "your aunt died a month ago, and when she was about to close her eyes, she said to your uncle, 'Miguel, if you see Luis again, ask him to forgive me.' Then she closed her eyes forever. A week after the funeral your uncle went back to Mexico."

"To what part of Mexico—do you know?"

"No, I don't."

"Don Juan, it is sad to know of all these things, but *Dios da y Dios quita*," I commented.

"Yes, Luis, that is life—God gives and God takes away," he repeated. Then he asked, "And what do you intend to do now?"

"I do not know, Don Juan. I would like to get a job somewhere, save money, and go to school."

"That is a very admirable ambition, but I think you are still too young to be able to get a job. However, you can go to the ore smelters every morning and stand by the gate to see if they will employ you. If they will hire you—for Christ sake tell them that you are eighteen years old. They need workers because the American Government is recruiting all the able-bodied young men for the army. The ore smelters are also going full blast. Think of it, Luis—in full force—three shifts—one from seven in the morning till three; the next from three to eleven at night; and the other from eleven to seven in the morning. They need workers badly, and besides that, the company is paying seven American pesos and forty-nine centavos for eight hours' work. Think of it! It is unbelievable. Seven dollars and forty-nine cents is good money for us poor devils." He paused for a moment, then said, "Luis, you can stay with us until you get a job, and after that you may do whatever you please."

"Thank you, Don Juan, you are very kind. Tomorrow I shall go and look for a job."

"That is right—you might just as well start at once," he stated. Then he called his wife and told her that I was going to stay with them for a while.

"Fine," said she; "he can sleep in the kitchen with the cat."

"Yes, Luis, you can sleep there with the cat. We will put a mattress on the kitchen floor for you," added Don Juan.

I thanked both of them for their generosity, and that evening I went to the main business section of town. Here I saw that there was a great deal of excitement about something. People were marching up and down the street, singing patriotic songs and carrying banners. Military bands were playing and the saloons were wide open. One of the Mexicans was reading aloud to another some signs which stated: "Do your bit for America!" "Save the world for democracy!" "Buy Liberty Bonds today, tomorrow will be too late!" "Do your part today—don't wait until tomorrow." Some of the people shouted, "Beat the Kaiser." "Down with Germany!"

I asked a Mexican fellow, who was standing by my side, *"Amigo, what is the occasion for this big celebration?"*

"This is not a celebration, *muchacho.*"

"What is it then?"

"Muchacho—Woodrow Wilson, the President of the United States, declared war against Germany the sixth of April of this year,

and ever since that day the people have been very excited over it," he explained.

"Ah, war here too, eh, *señor*?"

"Yes, war here too," he answered, and walked away

So after I had learned about the war situation I went to Don Juan's home to sleep in the kitchen with the cat. After making a very comfortable bed on the floor I undressed and lay down. As I was putting my head on my coat, which I had rolled to serve as a pillow, I whispered to myself, "Tomorrow will be another day."

26

The next morning, which was Friday, I went to look for work. I stood at the smelter gate for about an hour, but no one hired me. I went again and stood at the gate the second, the third, and the fourth day; still no one was interested in my services.

Finally, instead of my going to look for work in the morning or at the three o'clock shift, I went to the night one. While I was standing at the gate an elderly man came from the inside of the smelter yard and looked at the group of waiting men. Then he called one, then another, and still another; finally, pointing at me he asked, "How old are you, son?"

"Who, me?" I asked as I pointed to myself.

"Yes, you."

Immediately I answered, "I am eighteen years old—I will be nineteen next week."

"Good, you come with me. You want to work, don't you?" he asked.

"Indeed I do," I answered, and followed him.

After a few preliminaries at the ore smelter office, I was taken to the roasters. The roasters were large steel tanks, inlaid inside with white brick. There were twenty in all. Each tank had several flat divisions with a large hole in the center. Each tier was provided with three long steel-toothed arms attached to a perpendicular axle which extended through the center of the tank. The axle, in turn, was manipulated by means of electric motors, belts, pulleys, and gears. The crushed ore was deposited in the upper part of the tank, and when the axle revolved, the long steel-toothed arm raked the ore from the first tier to the second, and from the second to the third, and so on. As the ore dropped from tier to tier it was sprayed with burning oil in such a manner that when the raw metal reached the last tier it was red hot. From the roasters the red-hot ore was taken in four-wheeled tanks to the melting pots.

My job was to fill the wheeled tanks with hot ore. For the first few days I thought the job was quite hard and hot, but later I became used to it. The worst part of the work was the strong copper smoke which, in spite of our homemade masks, got into our lungs.

While working in the smelter, I met a Mexican who was an American citizen, and who spent most of his working time talking to me about Mexico. He was one of those Mexicans who had never been in Mexico, and longed very much to go there. One day he came to me and said, "Luis, I would surely love to go to romantic Mexico. Mexico— the land of dreams—romance music and beautiful *señoritas!*"

"Yes, my friend," I answered, "and don't forget that it is also the land of generals and revolutions."

"Ha-ha! That reminds me of a funny story I heard this morning about the Mexican army."

My friend started to laugh about the joke, and the boss, who was hiding and listening to us, came out and said, "Boys, I would like for you to do more work and less talking."

"Yes, sir," we answered, and started to work.

The next day my almost constant companion came to see me, and immediately started talking again about romantic Mexico. He asked me a lot of questions about the country. One of them was, "Luis, how much will it cost to go to Mexico?"

"It all depends—depends on the location and the time you want to spend there. Where would you like to go, and how long do you expect to remain in Mexico?" I asked.

"Well," he said, "not very far. Maybe as far as Hermosillo, Sonora, and stay there about three or four months."

"For that distance and that length of time, it will cost about two hundred dollars a person."

"Only two hundred dollars?"

"Yes, about that."

"Would you like to go to Mexico with me?"

"I don't have the money to spare."

"I mean, if I give you the two hundred dollars, would you like to go and show me the country?"

"I don't think so."

"Why?"

"Because I am very happy in the United States."

"Well, think it over," he said, and went to his work.

The next day he came as usual, and while I was filling one of the tanks with hot ore, he said, "Luis, here is your present."

"What present?" I asked.

Handing me a roll of bills, he answered, "The two hundred bucks I promised you." Then pausing for a moment while I looked at the money, he added, "Let us go to Mexico—what do you say?"

"When?" I asked.

"Next Sunday."

"No, that is too soon—it is Wednesday already."

"Why not right away? We don't have to wait for anything. We are getting paid in full today and we don't have to worry about nothing."

"Nevertheless, I think we should wait until a week from next Sunday."

"I don't think so. We can make what purchases we need within the next three days and leave Sunday."

"All right—have it your way," I said, putting the roll of bills in my pockets. "I will be ready to leave when you say."

"That is fine, and don't tell anybody about this," he said, as we sealed the bargain with a handshake.

The next day we did not come to work, and Saturday I bought a fifty-dollar black suit, a pair of shoes, several shirts, underclothes, and a black Stetson hat. The following morning about seven-thirty we were traveling on a bus to Naco, Sonora.

27

That Sunday, about three in the afternoon, my friend and I were at Naco, Sonora, boarding the passenger train to Hermosillo. In a little while the slow train was steaming its way to our destination While I was contemplating the panoramic view of the country, my friend took a large, official-looking envelope out of his inside coat pocket, and began tearing it to bits. As he was doing so he heaved a sigh of relief, and said, "Luis, I feel very safe, comfortable, and happy."

"Why, José?"

"Luis, I don't think you will be able to understand. You are still too young to know what this trip means to me," and opening the coach window he scattered the torn letter to the four winds.

"Well, José, you can at least tell me your troubles, even though I may not be able to understand them fully. Can't you?"

"Yes, I can. You see—I am an American citizen and once I was in the United States Regular Army. When I finished my enlistment term I received an honorable discharge, but I remained subject to be called for any emergency. Two weeks ago I received a letter from Washington demanding my services, that is, commanding me to report for duty." Then he paused for a minute, and turning away from me, continued, "Who in the hell wants to fight Germany? I am a Mexican—I am not a fighting man." Turning back to me, he asked, "Am I a fighting man? Answer me—am I?"

"I do not know, José. I don't even know anything about this citizenship business."

"I knew you would not understand. Moreover, you don't give a damn what may happen to me. You–"

"José, I am sorry," I interrupted.

"Sorry, hell! You do not know what fighting is, you are still a kid." Then grabbing his cap with his two hands and twisting it, he exclaimed, "I'll be damned if I die for anybody! I want to live and enjoy life. I want to get what is coming to me. I want to be free. Don't you?"

"Yes, I do, but I don't want to be a coward, or to be classified as one."

"I am not a coward, I am just sensible, and that is why I asked you to come with me and show me the country."

"Yes, José," I said, pointing to a green field, "Mexico is certainly a beautiful place for us Mexicans. Here is where we belong. That flowing river, that green forest, and those blue mountains were destined by God to provide beauty to this land of ours."

"Yes, and to hell with Uncle Sam."

"Who is Uncle Sam?"

"Don't you even know who Uncle Sam is?"

"No, I don't."

"Hell—Uncle Sam is—"

Our conversation was disturbed by the conductor, who came through the coach shouting the name of the approaching town.

Three days later we were walking the streets of Hermosillo in search of a place in which to live. We soon rented us a room very reasonably. The family was composed of three persons, the husband, wife, and a daughter. The girl was about fifteen years old and very attractive. She had a well-proportioned figure and it synchronized quite nicely with her coquettish ways.

For some unknown reason Consuelo, the daughter, fell in love with me, and to make things worse, my friend fell in love with her. Every day Consuelo would try to find new things to show me, and would take every opportunity to talk to me. Every day my friend was growing more jealous and bitter toward me, and more and more amorous toward the girl.

One day Consuelo asked, "Luis, what is the matter with José? Is he sick?"

"I do not know, Consuelo, but I know that you are beautiful," I told her.

"I don't believe you. I think you tell the same thing to all the girls you meet. Don't you?" And while talking to me she drew nearer, and I could see a passionate flame of love in her big brown eyes.

"Consuelo, I'm a boy of very limited experience. I want you to know that I have never had any girl, and I don't talk to anyone else but you. Besides that, you are more beautiful than anyone else I know. I can safely say that you are even more beautiful than the angels of heaven."

"Adorable liar—you have never seen the angels of heaven, have you? Have you?" she would ask, coming closer and closer toward me.

"Well—I—I guess not, but you surely look like one."

"It is not true—my mouth is very large and my lips are too thick."

"No, Consuelo, it is perfect—your lips match your pearly teeth."

"My eyes are too small and—"

"They are big enough to see me," I interrupted.

Pulling up a bit of the lower part of her gingham dress, she said, "Look—my legs are too skinny."

"Consuelo, I like skinny legs."

"And besides, the upper part of my body is out of proportion." Then, thrusting her shoulders backwards, she continued, "See, Luis—there is nothing much to me."

"Give it a chance, *chiquita*, it will develop. You are still too young."

"I am not young, I will be fifteen next—"

"Consuelo—Consuelo!" shouted her mother from the kitchen.

"Yes, Mamá," answered Consuelo.

"Come and wash the dishes. It is getting late."

"Yes, Mamá, I'm coming." Then she whispered to me, "Just to prove to you that I am not young, I am going to let you kiss me."

"Consuelo, where are you?" asked her mother.

"I'm coming, Mother," answered Consuelo, as I was about to kiss her. Then she whispered again, just before leaving, "Handsome one, I'll see you tonight—Mother is looking for me."

So my first romantic talk was spoiled by Consuelo's mother, and as I heard her call again, I said to myself, "Damned old bat! Why does she have to kill all the joy out of life?"

About a week later I came home from job seeking, and as I entered the door, Consuelo met me, and putting her hand in mine, she said, "Luis, tonight the Teatro Hidalgo is presenting the grand opera *Carmen,* and José wants me to go with him to see it."

"What is wrong with that?" I asked.

"Darling, I want to go with you."

"Well, if you want to go with me—with me you shall go."

"Good! You are sweet—I will be ready by seven-thirty," she

assured me.

So by eight-forty-five that evening, Consuelo and I were holding hands and listening to the melodious strains from the opera *Carmen.*

The next morning José was so angry at Consuelo and me that he called us every name he could think of but our own. Consuelo's mother heard the argument in our room, and she came to the door and knocked, asking, "What is all the swearing and noise about? This is a private house and not a barracks for soldiers."

José talked back to her, and as he finished saying what he thought of her and Consuelo, she shouted, "You couple of dirty rats! You get out of my house and stay out!" Then she ran back to the kitchen, shouting and crying, "Consuelo! Pedro! Antonio! Where are you? Call the police!"

But before the police came, my friend—now my enemy—and I got out of the place. And that day I took the train to Moreno, Sonora, and left my beloved Consuelo and that scoundrel of a José in Hermosillo.

28

Moreno, Sonora, is a mining town between Hermosillo and Guaymas. When I got off the train at Moreno I met a former comrade at arms. His name was Julián Castillo Dorado, better known in the company as *Borrachín*. He was a good man at heart, and an excellent gunner, but he had been discharged from the Contreras army for being a common sot, hence the nickname.

Once, when we were entrenched fighting the enemy, *Borrachín* turned his cannon and aimed at us, shouting, "Hey! *muchachos cabrones!* If you don't get down on your bellies I will let it go!"

Immediately some of us threw ourselves down, while others remained standing and shouting, "Don't do it, *Borrachín*." "You will be shot at sunrise for that, *Borrachín!*" "Don't be a damned fool, *Borrachín!*"

He would have discharged his cannon at us, but an officer knocked him over the head just before he pulled the trigger. After the battle, Julián Castillo Dorado was tried by a court-martial and dishonorably discharged from the army for drinking on the job and trying to cannonade us.

When *Borrachín* saw me getting off the train with my suitcase in hand, he asked, "Hello, *Coyote*, are you a general by now?"

"No, *Borrachín*, and I don't think I'll ever be one."

"Why not, *Coyote*? You are a damned good soldier."

"I was a soldier, I should inform you. About five months ago I was honorably discharged from the Contreras army."

"Honorably discharged?"

"Yes, honorably discharged," I parroted.

"That is more than I can say for myself. What are you going to do now that you are out of the army?"

"I don't know, *Borrachín*; I think I will go to Guaymas and go to school there."

"What the hell are you doing that for? Look at me, I never went to school and I am happy. Stay here and enjoy life. You can go with us to my ranch and look for gold."

"Who is us?" I asked.

"Me and my wife. After I was dishonorably kicked out of the army, I felt very bad about it, and so I got married."

"You got married, *Borrachín?*"

"Yes, *Coyote*, I married a girl who was educated in the convent. She plays the guitar and sings as well as I do. Every evening we have a good time singing. Her name is Mercedes. Come with us, *Coyote*. We are going to be away only a week, and you can help me drive my old Model T Ford. My wife's father gave it to us as a wedding present."

"I don't think that I should go. I want to go on to Guaymas as soon as possible."

"Come on, *Coyote*, be a good sport. It'll be only for a week. You are not in the army any more; you need a good vacation."

After he begged me so much I agreed to go with them. Immediately we purchased beans, flour, two prospector's pans, and some second-hand tools. Then we went to his place, where I met Mercedes, his wife. At his house I packed away my black suit and got my old clothes ready.

The following morning the three of us drove to the ranch, which was about ten miles from Moreno. Finally, after riding through rugged cactus-covered territory, over almost impassable roads, we stopped in front of a roofless adobe house.

"How do you like it?" *Borrachín* asked, as we were getting out of the battered Model T Ford. "This is my ranch!"

"Well, I—"

"It is not exactly a palace," he interrupted me, "but it is my house my ranch! I call it 'Las Tres Marías,' because my mamá was named María. My mamá's mama was called María, and my papá's mamá too was called María. That makes three Marías." After this he took me closer to his dilapidated house. As I looked in through a low window I found that it was inhabited by rattlesnakes, lizards, and God only knows what else. When I saw the intruders I asked, *"Borrachín*, are we going to live here?"

"No," he replied, "we are going to go over by the creek, where we can wash gold." Then pointing toward a high mountain, he continued, "My father used to tell me that those mountains made many poor Mexicans rich with gold."

After we had looked around, and had killed four rattlesnakes, two black scorpions, and a Gila monster, we drove across the creek, where Mercedes cooked a delicious snake soup spiced with chili sauce. She also made corn meal tortillas and fried beans with Mexican cheese for our lunch.

At Las Tres Marías, as *Borrachín* insisted on calling his ranch, we spent a great deal of time bringing dirt from the hills to the little running creek, where we panned it. But, regardless of the continuous hard work that the three of us did, we could realize only one third of an ounce of the yellow metal per day. That, we thought, was a very slow process of getting rich, so we decided to move to another spot where at least we could make a living wage.

While my friend and I were loading our camping outfit on the car, Mercedes filled one of the pans with dirt and went to the creek. A few minutes later, just as *Borrachín* was ready to call her to join us, she shouted, "Julián! Julián! Look! Come quick and see what found— gold!"

As we rushed to her, we saw that she was holding a bright yellow nugget as large as a medium-sized chicken's egg. Almost in unison her husband and I asked "Where did you get the dirt?"

"From the foot of that oak tree," she said, pointing excitedly with the piece of gold she held between he index finger and thumb.

At once *Borrachín* and I took a handmade wooden pick, an old shovel, our pans, and went to the tree. In about six hours' work we had dug from under the roots all the dirt which we thought had value. When we had finished panning it, my friend held before his unshaved brown face a glass fruit jar filled with gold dust, yellow grains and several large nuggets. As he stared at the container of precious metal, he beamed with joy and exclaimed, "*Amigos*, we are rich! Now we can go back to Moreno, and buy my wife all the things she needs in the house, and two gunny sacks full of beans for the winter. We can live a long time without working, I think!"

"Yes, and I can have my hair made curly at the beauty shop," said

Mercedes.

"And I can go to Guaymas as soon as we get back to Moreno," I remarked, as I began gathering wood to build an open fire to cook our supper.

The next day we awakened very early to fix our breakfast, and while eating it we looked toward the oak tree, which appeared as though it were a grotesque, mad spider balancing on all its legs getting ready to jump at somebody. After a few remarks about our good fortune, *Borrachín* decided to call the swaying tree "El Guardia del Tesoro Escondido."

"That is a very pretty name," Mercedes said. Then she repeated, "'The Guard of the Hidden Treasure!'"

By ten o'clock that morning we were on our way from *Borrachín*'s ranch to Moreno. While fording the creek we heard a loud explosion, then a prolonged diminishing hiss. As the hissing sound was gradually dying away, *Borrachín* pulled his faded straw sombrero over his ears and exclaimed, *"Carambas!* The rebels must be fighting again! Where is my rifle?"

"No rebels this time, Julián. It is only a blowout," commented his wife. And the three of us got out to fix the tire.

29

Two days after we had returned to Moreno we found that the three of us had panned twenty-five ounces of gold, for which we received five hundred Mexican pesos. My share of the money was one third; that gave me a nice nest egg on which to build my future. Then, in order to celebrate our good fortune, we had a little tamale fiesta at *Borrachín*'s house.

In the morning of the day we sold the gold, after we had purchased for the fiesta, *Borrachín* asked me to go with him to a wine shop. We soon found one which was called La Gran Mosca. As we entered the tavern a pretty, but quite dark, hostess came to greet us, saying, "Welcome to The Great Fly, *señores*."

When *Borrachín* saw the *señorita*, he asked, "Hello, my dark beauty, would you like to have a drink with us?"

The girl, in a sophisticated manner, without answering the question, said, *"Señor*, I was white once, but now I am dark because the sun has kissed me."

As the girl finished her statement, *Borrachín* held her hand and said, "I too was white once, *chiquita*, but look at me now! The damned sun has been kissing me too for the last thirty-two years, and now I am as black as—"

"What do you wish to drink, *señores*?" interrupted a young waiter, who started to clean the top of the table in the booth where we were sitting.

"Bring us three one-quart jugs of *pulque*, and a package of cigarettes," ordered *Borrachín*.

While the waiter went to fill the order, the girl talked us into buying two tickets for the national lottery, and having made the sale, she left us and went on to greet other customers.

In a few minutes the drinks were on the table and *Borrachín* took his jug, drinking the contents without stopping. When he was finished, he smacked his lips and said, "Ah, *pulque*, our Mexican beer, is the most wonderful drink in the world."

I sipped my drink, and it tasted slimy and had a nauseating odor; so I asked, "What is wonderful about it?"

"Why, *Coyote*, you don't know what is good. *Pulque* is the drink of the Mexican people," he replied, taking the jug from my hands and drinking most of it. Putting the container on the table he continued, "The *pulque* is made from the century plant, which is called maguey in the Indian language. The Indians thought that the plant bloomed only every hundred years, but in reality it blooms when it is between seven to ten years old. When the maguey is almost ready to blossom, the Indians cut out the stalk at the base of the plant, making a deep bowl in which the sap gathers. The juice runs so fast that one plant will furnish ten to fifteen pints of this delicious drink every day."

"How is it that you know so much about this fermented juice?" I asked.

"Well, *Coyote*," he said, taking the jug which was brought for the hostess, "my papa used to tell me the story of *pulque* and I know it by heart. Once upon a time, in the year 1050, I believe, a beautiful Indian maiden named Xochitl was on her way to Tula, the city of the emperor of the Toltecs."

At this point *Borrachín* drank half of the *pulque* out of the third jug before he continued, "Just think, *Coyote*! She was walking barefooted and on her head she was carrying a large narrow-mouthed pitcher."

Again *Borrachín* stopped and ordered another drink; then he drank the rest of the *pulque* which remained in the jug he had in his hands.

"When the damsel arrived at the gate of the palace, she told the servant that she had a present for the noble emperor," continued *Borrachín*, as he grabbed the refilled jug. "Just imagine, *Coyote*! She was taken right away to the ruler. Oh, *Coyote*, she was beautiful! While Xochitl, that is the name of the Indian maiden, remained standing before the emperor with the jar on her head, she appeared as innocent as a lamb. Her mouth was half open, her jet-black tresses hung over her shoulders, and her luminous eyes glared at the ruler."

"What did the emperor do when he saw Xochitl?" I asked.

After taking another drink, he answered, "The Indian chief greeted the maid kindly, and asked the nature of her visit. The girl, embarrassed and trembling, lowered the jar from her head and presented it to the emperor, explaining that the vessel contained the most delicious drink of the angels."

"Did he take it?" I asked.

"Did he take it?" repeated *Borrachín*. "Who wouldn't?"

"I don't know," I said.

"Yes, he took it," answered *Borrachín*, somewhat disgusted, then continued. "As the chief held the jar looking at the thick liquid, Xochitl said, 'Noble emperor, a child of the soil brings you the sweet water of the maguey, which, when blessed by the gods, becomes *pulque*. It is a liquor divine, which the angels in heaven prefer to wine.' At first the ruler was very dubious about the drink—just like you were. But since the girl standing before him looked so innocent and the odor of the beverage was so appetizing, he tasted it—like this," taking his own jug. "He found it sweet; then he looked at the girl and saw that she was charming. Then the emperor took another sip, like this," taking a drink himself. "And found the liquid mild and tasty. Again he looked at the girl, and saw that she was beautiful. The ruler took another drink, like this," sipping his, "and again he looked at Xochitl. He saw that she was more lovable than ever, and so he married her. Wasn't that wonderful? He married her."

By this time *Borrachín* was almost drunk, but he went on, "Yes, *Coyote*, he married her—and many, many days later, a very good-looking son was born to the emperor and Xochitl—and they called him Meconetzin, which means 'The son of the century plant.' Believe it or not, *Coyote*, but from that day on the clear sap of the maguey became the famous drink of the Mexican people—yes, *Coyote*, the drink of the people."

Then he gulped what *pulque* was in his jug and said, *"Coyote*, the people call me *Borrachín*, because I like *pulque*. I think I—hic—hic. I think I am drunk—hic. Yes, *Coyote*, hic, hic; I think—hic!"

"I think you are," I said. Then I called a carriage and took him home, where we had our fiesta.

That night *Borrachín* invited some of his friends to join us, and he related to them how we had killed several rattlesnakes, and how his industrious wife had cooked them to enrich our Mexican meals while we were placer mining. Our little social gathering was a very happy one. After the tamale dinner we sang and drank and I played the guitar.

The next morning I put on my black suit, took the train to Guaymas, Sonora, and left *Borrachín* and his wife in Moreno to enjoy their *frijoles*.

30

One day while I was walking along the piers in Guaymas, trying to make up my mind about whether I should stay there, I met my old friend the captain, who had taken me back to the caboose the time we burned the bridges when we were running away from the enemy. He was working in one of the warehouses, and as he saw me, he exclaimed, "Hey, *Coyote*, you little bastard! How are you? What are you doing here, and how is the army?" While shaking hands, he went on speaking, *"Coyote*, you look prosperous—how do you do it?"

"Well—fortune has been very kind to me, Captain."

"Don't call me captain, *Coyote*; call me Felipe—that is my name. *Carambas*, young fellow—I'm sure glad to see you. What are you doing?"

"I am looking for work."

"Are you broke?"

"No, not quite, but I have to work."

"Well, let me see. Can you come back at noon? I will take you then to meet Mr. Romero. He is the boss of Pier Four. He usually hires stevedores."

"Felipe, I am not strong enough to be a stevedore. I don't think I will be able to—"

"Don't worry, *Coyote*. He works for the Red Crown Gasoline Company, and he has lots of easy jobs. Yesterday he told me that he is expecting a shipment of gasoline, crude oil, and kerosene from Mazatlan. If you come *a las doce*, I'll take you to see him."

"Muy bien, I will come at twelve. Good-by, Felipe."

"Hasta la vista, Coyote," he shouted, as I went away.

At noon when I went back, Felipe was at Pier Four talking with Mr. Romero. At the warehouse, Felipe said to Romero, "This boy of whom I spoke to you—in the army we used to call him *El Coyote*, but his real name is Luis."

125

"How do you do, Luis?" asked Romero, shaking hands with me. "Do you want to work?"

"Yes, *señor*, I do."

"Fine. Come tomorrow at about seven-thirty and we will see what we can do for you."

I thanked Mr. Romero for his kindness; then Felipe and I went back to Pier Nine where he worked. On our way Felipe said, "I knew he would give you a job. He is a good man. You see, he is running around with my sister, and of course I think he is going to marry her. At least I hope so, because she likes him a lot." As he was telling me about Mr. Romero and his sister, the one o'clock whistle blew. Then he said, "Well, *Coyote*, I'll see you tonight." All of a sudden he asked, "Where are you staying, *Coyotito?*"

"I'm staying at Don Mariano's rooming house, and I like it there very much."

"That is fine—I'll see you tonight. Good-by, Luis."

"*Hasta la vista*, Felipe."

The next morning at seven-thirty I was at the warehouse waiting for Mr. Romero. On his arrival, he said, "Hello, Luis, how are you?"

"Very well, thanks, and how are you?"

"Oh, I have a beastly headache. I think I drank too much tequila last night." Then he asked, "Have you ever been in love?"

"Oh, yes, I have."

"It is terrible to be in love, because you never know whether the woman you love is in love with you," he said, sorrowfully.

"One never knows," I replied sadly.

"Well, Luis," he said, yawning, "I have an easy job for you. All you have to do is to check the boxes of kerosene and gasoline as they are brought in, or taken out. Do you know how to read?"

"No, *señor*, I don't."

"Well, you don't need to know. All you have to do is to put a vertical line in here for the gasoline and another here for the kerosene—like this," he explained.

"Very well, *señor* Romero, I understand."

"Good—here we work from eight in the morning until five in the afternoon. We take one hour for lunch, and the company pays one

American dollar for a day's work," concluded Mr. Romero. Then he took me to one of the doors of the warehouse, gave me paper and pencil, and again showed me how to mark the blanks.

That was the easiest job I'd ever had, and at the end of each working day the workers were paid as they signed out. I worked at that place for about two weeks. Then, one night while I was taking a walk around the depot and thinking about my Consuelo, I saw a number of families with bundles, trunks, and baskets of food, waiting in the station. One of the men told me that they were going to work in the United States.

"Who is taking all of you?" I asked him.

"Those Americans over there," pointing to three well-dressed men. "They are the bosses," he added. "Pánfilo, the interpreter calls them 'dee beega dee shots.'"

"Oh," I remarked. Then I went to see the three Americans, who were busy smoking, talking, and looking at some papers. When I came close to them I said, "*Señores*, 'dee beega dee shots,' *yo quiero trabajo.*"

They looked me over, and as they were doing so, Don Pánfilo, the interpreter, came and asked, "What do you want, *muchacho?*"

"I want work and to go to the United States with you."

As soon as I had finished my request, the interpreter turned toward the Americans, and said, "Deesa *muchacho*—boy wants *trabajo*—worka."

"Ask him if he has a family," said one of the "big shots."

After Don Pánfilo had asked me the question, he said to the three bosses, "No—yes, hee—shee no *tiene*—has no *familia.*"

"Ask him if he wants to take a job for a year picking cotton in Arizona, at four cents a pound."

Don Pánfilo again asked me the question, and as I said "*Sí,*" he mumbled to the Americans, "*Sí*—yes," moving his arms and pointing at me. "Deesa *muchacho*—boy shee could tooka dee joba—*trabajo* peekin' cotton—*algodón.*"

"Fine, fine. Tell him to be here tomorrow morning ready to take the eight o'clock train to Nogales," said one of the recruiting men to Don Pánfilo, who in turn translated the message to me.

That same night I went to Don Mariano's rooming house and got my only blanket, my suitcase, and my black suit. From there, I went to the depot and slept in the station waiting room because I was afraid of being left behind.

The next day, about twelve-thirty, when we were passing through Hermosillo, I wanted to get off to see my Consuelo, and tell her good-by, but of course I could not leave the train.

31

The twenty-fifth morning of November, 1918, the families and I were in the United States immigration office at Nogales, patiently waiting to be examined by the officials. When my turn came, the person who examined me said, "Young man, let it be known that you are entering the United States of America to pick cotton and to work as a farm hand for the term of one year. At the end of a year you shall return to Mexico. This is in accordance with the laws adopted by Congress and enforced by the Department of Labor of the United States." Then he took a form from his desk and the regular routine of questioning began. When he had finished asking questions and filling the blank spaces, he said, "Raise your right hand."

By mistake I raised my left hand.

"Your right hand," he commanded.

When I had my arm up in the air, he said, "Repeat with me: 'I, the undersigned, do solemnly swear that the statements made by me in answer to the foregoing questions are full and true to the best of my knowledge and belief. So help me God.'" Then he asked me to sign the documents, which I did by making a cross as a signature.

By three in the afternoon of the same day, our fast train was speeding its way through the Arizona desert to Phoenix. We arrived at the capital of the state late that night, and our coach was uncoupled and switched onto a side track. In the morning, when we got out of the coach, the "big shots" were nervously walking about with other well-dressed men. Don Pánfilo followed them like a faithful dog after his master. At about ten in the morning a lot of farmers came to the station driving old carts, buggies, and "flivvers." The farmers would talk with the "big shots," and after a short conversation they would sign some papers, and would come to where we were, pointing, "I want these these—and these." Then they would take with them three or four of the families.

Somewhere about three in the afternoon I noticed a tall, red-faced man driving a beautiful team of black horses hitched to a four-wheeled rack. When he had pulled the restless animals to an abrupt stop, the three bosses greeted him, and one of them said, pointing to us, "Benson, this is all we have left. You came too late."

Mr. Benson jumped off the cart and asked, "Do all these children belong to one family?"

"No," said one of the men who greeted him. "Those six over there belong to this man and this woman. This boy here is alone," he said, touching my shoulder. Then he pointed to a young man, who was seated on his suitcase, and said, "He is single."

"Benson, I think you should take all of them to your ranch," suggested one of the partners.

"I guess so," mumbled Mr. Benson. After he had signed the papers to own us, he came to each one of the workers, and asked, "Do you speak English?" When the person who was questioned said, "No, *señor*, me no espeaka dee Eengleesh," then Mr. Benson would say, "*Mucho malo, mucho malo*—too bad." When he asked me the question, I answered, "No, *señor, yo no hablo inglés.*" Immediately Don Pánfilo, who was standing near by, said to Mr. Benson, "Deesa *muchacho*—boy hee says hee no espeaka da Eengleesh."

"*Mucho malo, mucho malo,*" repeated Mr. Benson. To that I said, "Oh, no, *señor*, me no *mucho malo*—yo estrong—me wanta worka."

"Fine, fine," he said, and laughed.

The reason why I was able to say "strong," "wanta," and other words, was because Don Pánfilo was teaching me English the way he had learned it. The first night we were on the train he had said to me, "Luis, I like you, and I am going to tell you something that is going to be for your own good. You might just as well know that the only way you can get a good job in the United States is by knowing how to speak English." Then, holding the upper part of the lapels of his blue jumper, he continued, "Look at me, I have a good job—I espeaka da Eengleesh. There is no Mexican in the United States to espeaka da Eengleesh the way I do. I can read it, write it, and teach it. Yes, I can teach it, and because you have been such a good fellow, I am going to teach it to you in ten lessons so you can get a good job in the United States like the one I have. I got a good job."

While he was parading up and down the aisle like a proud peacock, telling me what a good job he had, and bragging about his good fortune, a fellow countryman, who was reading a newspaper, asked, "Say, Don Pánfilo, if hot air and gas makes balloons go up, what in the name of *Jesucristo* holds you down?"

"His big belly keeps him anchored to the ground," shouted an old man, who was eating a piece of dry bread.

At this last remark the crowd laughed, and Don Pánfilo said to me, "Don't pay any attention to them fellows. All they like to do is to eat and to make foul remarks. They will never amount to anything." Then he proceeded, "The only way you can learn English in ten lessons is by reading a book like this," and taking a small dictionary from his pocket, he pointed, "You see—you read the Spanish word and then the English. After you have learned both words you pronounce them like this: '*Beso*—kees,' '*Señorita*—meess,' and so on. Is it not simple? The English language is one of the easiest languages to master. I have tried all the languages—yes—all of them." Suddenly he asked, "Can you read?"

"No, I can't."

"Oh, well, you have to learn to read before you can speak any language. However, you are young, and you can learn. I can teach you a few words—I am a good teacher." In this manner he proceeded to instruct me in the art of learning to speak English in ten lessons; thus I was able to talk to Mr. Benson.

The first afternoon at the ranch, Mr. Benson gave the family a large tent, and a small one to the single man and me. Then he issued us a ration of groceries and let us use some old cooking utensils which were stored in the barn.

The next morning our employer took us to the cotton field and taught us the proper method of removing the wool-like material from the pod. He said, "You should be able to pick from a hundred to a hundred and fifty pounds a day. The more cotton you pick, the more money you'll get. Go to it and make a fortune."

The first day I picked only seventy pounds and the boss said, "*Mucho malo.*"

The following day I picked a little more, and by the end of the cotton season I was able to pick ninety-five pounds per day.

After the cotton season was over, we stayed on the ranch to cultivate the fields for the following year.

By the middle of March of 1920, I told Mr. Benson that since I had been with him over a year I wanted to go back to Mexico. He said, "Luis, you may do as you please. Come to my office and I will go over your account." In the office he continued, "Luis, you came to my ranch the twenty-sixth of November 1918, I paid the recruiting men thirty dollars for your train fare and the food you ate on the way. I gave them eight dollars for the immigration fees. Now you owe me seventy-five dollars for food and shelter, twenty-three dollars for clothes, and twenty dollars that I have given you in cash. Let me see." Mumbling between his teeth, he added, "Thirty, plus eight, plus seventy-five—twenty-three and twenty is forty-three. Well, well, well—you owe me exactly one hundred and fifty-six dollars. Now we take this amount from the money you have earned, which is—let me see six from eight—two, seven and one eight, and two is—well, well, well—you have ten dollars coming to you."

"The whole amount of ten dollars!" I exclaimed.

"Yes, ten dollars."

"For a moment I thought I was going to owe you ten dollars."

"Oh, no! I am very honest—I don't steal money from anybody."

"Thank you, Mr. Benson. And may I have my ten dollars."

"Yes, of course. Here they are and if you ever want to come back to work for me, you are welcome to do so."

I thanked Mr. Benson again and left his ranch with my ten dollars, my blanket, my suitcase, and my black suit. Later I found that Mr. Benson, the honest man, had cheated me out of the greater part of my wages.

From the ranch I went to Phoenix, and after a few days in the capital of the state, I went to Glendale, Arizona.

32

In Glendale I worked one month as a shepherd, taking care of two hundred and thirty sheep. I liked that job very much, but the owner of the flock discharged me because, through my carelessness, the wolves killed some newborn lambs. After that I did odd jobs as a farm hand on different ranches.

One hot day in the month of June 1920, while I was dozing on the steps of the cabin where I was staying, suddenly I heard a voice that asked in Spanish, "Young man, have you found the Lord?"

When I raised my head I saw a pretty lady about thirty years of age. "When did he disappear?" I asked. "I didn't know that he was lost again."

"Oh, excuse me—are you a Christian?"

"I—I guess so. I am not an animal. You see we Mexicans believe that since we are born of humans, we are born Christians."

"Yes, young man, but do you know the Lord Jesus Christ, Who died for us? Has He come to your heart? Have you found Him?"

"Oh, I beg your pardon, *señorita*. For a moment I thought you meant whether I had found the landlord. You see, he got lost the other day, and I thought he had disappeared again."

"No, the Lord I'm talking about is the Savior. The Omnipotent Son of God Who died on the cross to save us sinners."

"Who is us, may I ask?"

"All of us. You, I—we are all sinners by nature, but the Lamb of God cleanses us from all sin."

"I don't think I am a sinner. I don't smoke, don't drink, don't steal. I haven't killed anybody—I lie, but my lies don't hurt anyone. I love the beautiful *señoritas*, but I don't think that is a sin, is it?"

"Do you go to church?"

"No, I don't. I don't believe what the priest says."

"Do you belong to any church?"

"Well, ye–ye–e–no, I don't."

"Why don't you come to the mission tonight? We sing, pray, and drink hot coffee. Come tonight, will you? The Lord will be waiting for you there." Then she gave me a personal card, and added, "You will find me here. This is the mission's address. I live there also—my name is Magdalene Smith. Come to the mission tonight."

As she was leaving, I said, "I will be there, Miss Smith, since you and the Lord will be waiting for me."

At about eight by the clock that night, I was listening to some testimonials, and later enjoyed the hymn that the congregation sang. When the service was over, Miss Smith came to me and said, *"Señor* Pérez, I'm glad you came. Did you like the singing?—do you sing? I know all the Mexican people like to sing and most of them have good voices."

"Señorita Smith, I don't sing."

"Can you read? You may take this Bible if you like."

"Thank you, *señorita,* but I do not know how to read."

"Oh, how sad! What are you doing tomorrow?"

"I do not know—I think I will have to go out and look for work."

"If you don't find a job, will you come to see me?"

"I guess so," I said.

She extended her hand. "I'll be waiting for you, and don't worry, Brother Pérez. 'All things work together for good for them that love God.'"

"I am not worrying, Miss Smith."

"I'm glad, Mr. Pérez—good night."

"Hasta la vista, Miss Smith."

The next day after I came back from job hunting, I went to the mission, and Miss Smith asked me a lot of questions about my past. When I had told her some of my experiences in Mexico, she asked, "Brother Pérez—and now that you are in the United States, what do you intend to do? What seems to be your greatest ambition?"

"I do not know what I will do, Miss Smith, but my greatest desire is to save my money and go to a school somewhere. I want to learn something, and I want to do useful things."

"Brother Pérez, if you believe in the Lord Jesus Christ, you will be able to go to a school." After pausing for a second, she asked, "Are you baptized?"

"I guess I am—I think I was baptized as a child."

"Well, except a man be baptized in the name of the Lord he cannot enter the Kingdom of Heaven. You have to be converted from paganism and heresy to Christianity. Will you be baptized?"

"I do not know."

"Yes, Brother—be saved! Today is Tuesday and next Sunday some of our brethren are going to be baptized. Will you be one of them?"

"Perhaps," I said, as she extended her hand to tell me good-by.

The following Monday I was suffering from a terrific cold which I caught as the result of having been submerged in a tank of cold water. As the minister held the end of my nose while I was being thrown backward into the tank of icy water, he said, "I baptize thee, Brother Pérez, 'In the name of the Father, the Son, and of the Holy Ghost'—Amen!" So from that day on I was a baptized Christian.

One day during the month of August of the same year, while I was at the mission, Miss Smith said, "Brother Luis, I have some good news for you."

"What is it, Miss Smith?"

"I found a very good school in Albuquerque, New Mexico; the rates are very reasonable. You can go there for only seventy-five dollars for nine months. That includes tuition, board, and room."

"But I don't have the seventy-five dollars—I have only sixty-five."

"Don't worry, Brother Luis. The church and a lady—that is, a teacher who teaches in one of the Oklahoma high schools—are going to help you to pay the tuition for the first year. The money you have will be enough to pay your train fare. You must leave here by the first of next month. I have already made reservations for you in the school. Somebody will come to meet you there."

"Thank you, *señorita,* you are very kind. May I kiss your hand?"

"No, Christian people should never kiss."

I thanked Miss Smith again, and by the second of September I was on my way to the school in Albuquerque.

33

I arrived at Albuquerque the fifth day of September at about three in the afternoon. When I got off the train, an old man greeted me in Spanish, saying, "How do you do—are you Mr. Pérez?"

"Yes, *señor*, I am Luis—Luis Pérez," I replied.

"My name is George Williams—Dr. Williams. I am the dean of the school. We have a very nice private institution. Did you enjoy your long trip?"

"Yes, *señor*, I did."

"Miss Smith wrote me that you have no parents. Is that right?"

"That is true, Dr. Williams."

"Well—I hope you will have a good time here with us. We are just like one big happy family. The school is three miles south of the city. I don't mind driving from the place to town because this is a good horse. We will be there in no time. Classes will start tomorrow morning." Thus he rumbled, and eventually he asked, "Have you ever been in school before?"

"Yes, *señor*, about a week when I was nine years old."

"Well, I think we will have to give you an entrance examination to determine the grade you should be in now. How old are you?"

"I was sixteen the twenty-fifth of last month."

"Do you see those white buildings over there?" Pointing toward the south, he explained, "That is our college. We are going to have a big crowd this year."

"How many pupils do you usually have, Dr. Williams?"

"It varies. The year before last we had seventy-five. Last year we had only forty-nine. This year I expect we will have about eighty boys, besides a few girl day students. That is a good number."

"What else do pupils do other than study?"

"There is always a great deal to be done around the school. Since the parents of the pupils don't pay us enough to hire someone to do the work, the children usually have to help in the kitchen. Some of the older boys take care of the horses and cows. The pupils also sweep the school rooms and do various jobs around the place. Quite often some of the students are able to get work after school hours or on Saturdays, in private homes."

"I hope I will be able to do something like that because I am short of money."

"I hope so. I will see that you get a job, but don't neglect your school work because that is the most important thing." Suddenly he shouted, "Whoa, Betsy! Here we are, Luis. This is our home. I will take you to your room and introduce some of the boys to you."

"Thank you, Dr. Williams," I said. Then I was taken to my room where I met a lot of little and big boys. They were very pleasant and friendly, and every one of them wanted me to go to see his room. The bigger fellows wanted me to go out to try to make the basketball team, the baseball team, and the many other ball teams they had in the school.

After dinner the registrar of the college came to my room and asked, "Well, sir—do you speak English?"

"No, *señor*, I don't."

"In that case we will have to do all our talking in Spanish."

"I think so, *señor*," I replied.

"Did you enjoy your trip?"

"Yes, *señor*, I did."

"Fine, fine! What school did you attend last, and when?"

"I haven't attended any school—that is, I—I went to a Mexican parochial school for a week when I was nine years old."

"Is that all the education you have had?"

"Yes, *señor*."

"Do you know how to read and write?"

"No, *señor*."

"How old are you?"

"Sixteen."

"Where were you born?"

"In San Luis Potosí, Mexico."

"Are your father and mother living?"

"No, *señor*, they are dead."

"Can you spell 'college'?"

"I think so—let me see—c-o-l-e-g-e."

"No, college has two l's. Can you spell school?"

"I think not, *señor*."

"Well, Luis—Luis is your name, isn't it?"

"Yes, *señor*, Luis Pérez is my name."

"I think you will have to start from the beginning. That is, you have to start in the first grade. There you will have to learn to read, write, and do some simple problems in arithmetic. It is too bad that you have to be with the little children, but it is necessary that you know your a-b-c's before entering into higher learning Well, tonight we are having a community sing. It is compulsory—you better be there."

"Yes, *señor*, I will be there."

"Do you sing?"

"No, *señor*, I don't."

"What can you do, anyway?"

"Nothing, I guess."

"Do you like music?"

"Yes, I do."

"All right, you come to the community singing—I am the leader of it."

He went out and left me alone wondering whether I should have come to the school. When he was away from the building, some of the older boys came in and one of them asked, "What did the old crank tell yuh?"

"He is mean," said another boy. "Sometimes he sends us to bed without supper. Ain't it the truth, fellows?"

"Yeah, he is mean," shouted the crowd of boys.

A third boy remarked, "His wife left him because he sleeps with his mouth open and snores."

"Nyeah," said still another kid, talking through his nose. "He teaches history and he expects us fellows to read a chapter in the red history book in ten minutes. He is a lousy teacher. He was a garbage collector before he was hired by the school to teach history. Ain't it so, fellows?"

"Yeah," cried the boys.

"The Bull!" shouted one of the boys, and at that all of them ran out.

In a few minutes another teacher, known to the boys as "The Bull," stuck his head into my room and asked, "Is it warm enough for you?"

"Yes, sir," I answered, and he went away.

At a quarter to eight that night we were singing patriotic and religious songs. The principal of the school delivered a speech in Spanish; then it was translated into English. The college was an American school, but two thirds of the pupils were Mexicans. Our studies were in English, but we spoke Spanish on the campus.

Somewhere about a quarter to nine we were in our rooms, and at nine o'clock a boy rang a large bell.

"What is that for?" I asked one of my roommates.

"Every night at nine that bell is rung, and that means that we should kneel and say our prayers. Five minutes from now the bell is rung again, and that means to undress and go to bed. At nine-thirty the bell rings and the lights go out. At six tomorrow morning the principal of the school pulls the rope of the bell, and that means to get up. We do everything here by bells. You have to get used to it."

Soon the nine-thirty bell was ringing and the boy continued, "Good night, Luis. In the morning I shall tell you more about the different school rules and class regulations. I have been here nine years."

"Nyeah," snuffled the other roommate, "he has been here nine years and he is still in the sixth grade."

"Shut up, snuffler!" said the boy who had explained the rules; and just then the teacher in charge of the dormitories came by and said, "No more talking, boys—nine-thirty already."

"Good night, Luis," whispered one of the boys, and after that everything was silent.

34

During the summer vacation following my second year in school, I received a letter from Miss Smith, the missionary. She informed me that she was going to move to Los Angeles, California. She said that she was going to teach music in a Spanish seminary and also she added, "Brother Luis, if you still have the intention of becoming a minister of the Lord, as you said you did, you should come and enter the seminary. I have already talked to the dean, and he tells me that he can find work for you to do while attending school. It is a fine place; the teachers and the students are all fine Christian people. I hope you will come. I will be there in the school and once near you I could help you with your English—particularly letter writing—your Spanish, and your music. Think it over and let me know. I shall send you my Los Angeles address as soon as I can."

I had not answered Miss Smith's letter when I received another urging me to come, sending me her new address and instructions as to how to get there.

I wrote Miss Smith as soon as I could and told her that I was more than glad to come to Los Angeles, to enter the seminary and become a minister of the Lord to preach the Gospel to the Mexican people.

On the thirteenth of September, 1922, I arrived in Los Angeles. I followed Miss Smith's directions to the letter. On the train I wore my black suit, red tie, and tan button shoes. By this time my one and only suit was a pitiful sight. I had outgrown it. The coat sleeves barely covered my elbows. The legs of the trousers were also very short, but worst of all, the seat had been patched several times. The whole suit looked awful and I was aware of the fact, but there was nothing that I could do to improve it. When I wore it around people, I had to sit down or find a way to walk backwards, or behind the crowd, in order to keep them from criticizing my antiquated pantaloons.

Miss Smith had instructed me to come to the seminary as soon as I arrived in Los Angeles. She assured me that she would be at the institution when I came. When I got off the train I called a taxi and told the driver where I wanted to go. In less than three minutes the cab stopped in front of the seminary, and the driver said, "Here we are, and here is your ticket. Thirty cents, please."

"Thirty cents for this short ride?" I asked.

"That is what the meter shows."

After I had paid my fare, I went to the door and found it locked. Then I went next door, which was the missionaries' residence, and after I had knocked, there came a whizz from a little unfamiliar funnel-shaped pipe that was next to the door frame. After the whizzing sound I heard a voice which asked, "Who is it?"

I was so surprised by this contraption that I did not answer the question. Again I heard the whizzing and a second, "Who is it?" This time I gained a little courage and came closer to the pipe and said, "Eet ees I."

After a few seconds a blue-eyed, Amazon-type young woman came to the door and questioned me, "What can I do for you?"

"Ees Mees Esmeeth, shee reeves here, yes, no?"

"No Mees Esmeeth, shee no reeves here," she answered, mimicking my broken English. Then she laughed and asked, "Are you Luis?"

"Yes, *señorita,* I am Luis," I answered, smiling.

"Miss Smith asked me to tell you that she had to go to a faculty meeting, and that she wants you to wait for her. in the next building. She has been telling me a lot of nice things about you. Did you enjoy your trip?"

"Yes, *señorita,* I did."

"Wait for me here. I am going to get the key to open the seminary door," she said, letting me in and pointing to a chair in the waiting room.

When my hostess returned with the keys we went to the seminary. And while we were in the main hall of the institution, she said, "Luis, you may wait here for Miss Smith. She'll be in shortly. My name is Caroline Olson. I'm one of the missionaries on the faculty. I live next door and I am in charge of the clinic and the commissary of the seminary. Every year we give a lot of baskets of food to the needy." After a short pause she continued, "I hope you will enjoy your school work here. We will be very glad to help you in every way we can. Now I must go; I have to fix my dinner and after that I have to call on the sick. Good-by, Luis, I will see you later."

"Good-by, Miss Olson, I hope that I will see you often," I said, as she was going out of the building. She was so charming that I fell in love with her at first sight.

That night the men at the dormitories told me that Miss Olson was the best-looking missionary in Los Angeles. They said that many of the students had been trying to make a date with her, but not one of them had had any luck.

My first semester in the seminary was the hardest, but Miss Olson, who was my inspiration, made me forget my troubles. In fact, I was the fortunate man who won her affections.

One bright afternoon, while I was alone in the seminary library, she tiptoed her way to me, and when I noticed her, she asked, "Will it be possible for a lady to visit a man who is alone?"

"Why not? Especially when the man who is alone is in love with the *señorita* who comes to visit him."

"But what if we are seen together?"

"Don't be afraid, *señorita*. I can always say that you are a beautiful Christian missionary who came to bring good tidings of great joy to a lonely pagan."

"That is enough out of you, 'Lonely Pagan.' I came to ask if you would like to go to a concert with me tonight."

"And will you take me to dinner also?" I asked, jokingly.

"Of course, it is understood—I expect you to feed me and entertain me whenever you take me out, but this is my treat tonight."

When I heard her statement I stood close to her and said, "*Señorita* Olson, you are certainly kind and beautiful. Your eyes are so blue and tempting that I wish I could kiss them."

"You must not say that. When temptation comes to you, you should say, 'Get behind me, Satan.'"

"Oh, no, *señorita*, I can never say that. I always say, 'Come close to me, you little devil,'" and as I said that I embraced her and kissed her lips. That was the beginning of a romance, and after that we went together to many interesting places.

One night during the Christmas vacation of 1923, I was with Miss

Olson in the seminary storeroom, helping her to put up the baskets of food for charity. While we were there I kissed her. Miss Olson and I never thought anything of our kiss. But it so happened that Mr. Mingles, who taught logic in the seminary, was also in love with Miss Olson, and at the moment when I kissed her, Mr. Mingles went by the outside of the building and saw our silhouettes through the frosted glass window. He managed to call the dean's attention to his observation of our lovemaking.

Three days after I had kissed my blue-eyed missionary, I was summoned into the dean's office.

35

When I entered the dean's office I noticed that he was sitting in the center of the room, surrounded by the faculty of the seminary, with the exception of Miss Smith. The dean ordered me to sit down and as I was doing so, he said, "Mr. Pérez, we have a very grave matter to discuss with you. I have reports that you have misbehaved and that your conduct has been shameful."

"Is that right?" I asked.

"Yes, that is right. Three weeks ago I saw you in Westlake Park walking arm in arm with Miss Olson."

"That is true; and last week I saw you on Fifth Street walking arm in arm with—"

"That is no concern of yours," he interrupted me.

"May I say that same thing to you about Miss Olson and myself?"

"Mr. Pérez, three days ago Mr. Mingles saw you kissing Miss Olson. Is it true?"

"Is it a crime for a man to kiss the woman he loves?"

"Did you kiss Miss Olson?" he shouted.

"Yes, sir, I kissed Miss Olson. Do you have any objections to that?"

"Mr. Pérez, I want you to know that this is a seminary for gentlemen—for ministers of the Lord, and not for incorrigible and irresponsible young men such as you. People are talking about the institution and we are losing their respect. Mr. Mingles was very much disturbed and mortified in knowing how the pupils of this great institution of learning have been carrying on with the workers of the Lord. You either have to stop seeing Miss Olson or else we'll have to take other means to settle these things which are so annoying to the faculty of a Christian school."

"Is Mr. Mingles the spy of the seminary?" I asked.

"I'm not a spy, young man—I want you to know that I was only doing my duty," said Mr. Mingles angrily.

"If you are not a spy, how can you say that I was kissing Miss

144

Olson?"

"Because I saw your silhouettes through the frosted glass windows Saturday night," said Mr. Mingles, shaking his finger at me.

"And how can you prove that the silhouettes you saw were ours?"

"Because I stayed outside of the building until you two came out of the storeroom."

"Heh-heh-heh," laughed a very elderly teacher, who heretofore had been reading his Bible.

"Mr. Mingles," I continued, "that proves that you are not only a spy, but also a tattletale and stool pigeon. I feel sorry for Miss Olson because her reputation is at stake, but if she is willing, I am going to keep on seeing her—and—kissing her. Neither the dean, the tattler, nor the faculty of the seminary can stop a man from caring for a woman. Gentlemen—I love Miss Olson. Is that clear? I love her!"

I was so angry that I could have called them worse names than the ones the wounded sergeant called the Moralistas the night I was trying to bring him into our trenches.

The dean was so enraged at what I said that he got up and shouted, "Mr. Pérez! You will have to apologize to Mr. Mingles and to all of us, or else you will be expelled from the institution!"

"*Señor* dean, I thank God that this is not the only, school in the United States. If I am expelled from here because I love a woman, I consider myself very fortunate. Besides, *señor* dean, I don't have to apologize to Mr. Mingles nor to—"

"You are expelled from the seminary!" he roared a the top of his voice, interrupting me.

"Thank you, *señor* dean," I said, and made a slight bow and walked backwards to the office door. Then stopped and added, "Good-by— Christian friends!" and I walked out.

I went at once to the dormitories and picked up my belongings, including my black suit, that is, the remains of a suit—the vest and the coat.

Miss Smith interceded for me, and the following week the dean asked me to come back. I returned to the school, but I was not very happy there. Most of the teachers and students treated me coldly.

When Miss Olson knew that I had been expelled from the seminary because of our romance, she worried so that she became ill. I did not see her for about a month, and of course that made me feel very miserable. There was nothing I could do; I was so closely watched by the members of the faculty that I had to be extremely careful. By the end of the summer semester of 1924 I decided to quit the seminary for good. While I was pondering over the possibility of leaving the school, I was able to take Miss Olson out to dinner. I was very glad to see and talk to my beloved one. When I had a chance I said, "Caroline, darling, I love you. Will you marry me?"

"Luis, I love you very much, but I love you as though you were my brother; and I wish that you could love me in the same way."

"No, Caroline, I could not love you that way. I have always loved you as a man loves a woman. I fell in love with you the first time I saw you. I love you and want you to marry me."

"Luis, what will my people think if I marry you? You don't have a job, and you are too young yet. We wouldn't be happy—no, darling, we wouldn't be happy. You understand, don't you?"

"Yes, Caroline, I understand—I guess we wouldn't be happy. Shall we go?"

I was brokenhearted, but a week after our dinner date I saw Miss Olson again. She said, "Luis, I have some news for you."

"News for me?" I asked. "Are you going to marry me?"

"No, you silly boy, I would love to marry you, but you know as well as I do that we could never be happy, and—"

"And what?" I interrupted her. "Is it because you are ten years older than I am?"

"Ten years would make a lot of difference," she said, trying to look stern; then her voice broke and sobbingly she whispered, "Luis, darling, I love you—I cannot think straight—forgive me. I am not able to stand this ordeal any longer, and I have resigned my post as a missionary. Tomorrow evening I am going home. Will you take me to the station? I want you to be a man and face your troubles as I am going to face mine."

"Caroline, I will do everything you have asked me to do. I know I will miss you, but your wish is to go—and you shall go."

The next evening the school faculty came to the station to see Miss

Olson off. After bidding them good-by, she kissed me a fond farewell in their presence; then she climbed into her coach.

"How scandalous!" mumbled a member of the faculty, as Miss Olson kissed me.

"Disgusting!" exclaimed another.

The conductor shouted, "All-l-l aboard!" and in a few minutes Caroline was gone.

While we were in the station after Miss Olson had gone, I told the dean that I was going to leave the seminary. I also said, "*Señor*, I don't think I was ever cut out to be a minister of the Lord."

"Mr. Pérez," he replied, "you haven't been called by the Lord yet to be one of His ministers. Pray, pray, and pray without ceasing to the Mighty God for understanding, for guidance, and for forgiveness."

"Thank you, *señor* dean," I said; then I left him and some of the members of the faculty in the station and went to the dormitories to get my belongings. This time I left my black suit in the rag bag.

36

By the early part of September, 1924, I had saved ninety-five dollars, and a friend of mine owed me thirty. With a hundred and twenty-five dollars to my credit I decided to enroll in a public school.

When I was in the seminary doing missionary work I had met a Mexican who was staying in a private home owned by a widow. And when I was looking for a place to stay, I came upon the Mexican again and told him that I was going back to school.

"Back to the seminary?" he asked.

"No, I am going to try my luck in a public school this time. No more seminary for me; I have had enough of it."

"Well, I wish you luck, but it takes money to live while attending school."

"That is true, and my mission just now is to look for a cheap place in which to live."

"Why don't you come to the house where I'm staying? The landlady is an American woman, and a very good Christian. She might let you have a corner of a room, and board for a very reasonable amount. Come over tonight and meet her."

"All right, Pedro, I'll be there," I said to my friend as I took leave of him.

That evening I went to visit Pedro's landlady, and after I had heard a long discourse upon the divinity and resurrection of the crucified Christ, and the purity of the Virgin Mary, the owner of the house concluded by saying, "Young man, seeing that you are a Christian boy, saved by the precious blood of the Lamb of God, I'm going to let you share one of my rooms and have two meals a day for the nominal price of fifteen dollars per month. I love the Mexican people and I want to help them. Now, shall we bow our heads and thank God for His kindness?"

"Hallelujah! Praise be His Holy Name by every tongue in His universe," mumbled my friend Pedro, while the landlady finished by repeating the Lord's Prayer in a very high-pitched voice.

On the sixteenth day of September, 1924, I was eating a hamburger sandwich at a little counter near the Hollywood High School. Sitting next to me was an elderly gentleman eating a rather sumptuous meal. As he was served, he turned to me and asked, "Young man, will you pass the salt?"

"Yes, *señor, con mucho gusto.*"

He looked at me, asking, "So you speak Spanish, eh?"

Yes, *señor, soy Mexicano.*"

"You are a Mexican—fine, fine. I talk to you in Spanish. I'm a Spanish teacher in the Hollywood High School, but I seldom find anyone who knows the language."

After a short pause he asked, "What is your name?"

"Luis Peréz."

"What do you do for a living?"

"Cement mixer. That is, I have been working for a contractor, building concrete sidewalks."

"How interesting!"

"Not to me."

"Don't you have some kind of a trade?"

"No, *señor*, I don't."

"Have you finished high school?"

"I do not know what you mean by high school." Then I told him about my previous education, and also that I wished to attend some public school.

"Well, I doubt very much whether you'll be able to enter any public school."

"Why, *señor?*"

"Because you don't have the credits demanded by the public-school system. However, you can come with me to the school and we will talk to the principal. He is a very fine man. We like him very much."

"I will be glad to go with you right away," I said eagerly.

"Not so fast, son. Wait until I eat this delicious beef steak."

After the Spanish teacher had finished his dinner both of us went to the school office. While we were going through the hall of the administration building he said to a man whom we met, "This boy wants to enroll in the school, but he doesn't speak English very well, and he doesn't have any public-school credits. He is also twenty years old."

The man whom we met looked me over and said to the Spanish teacher, in a rather serious tone of voice, "Give him a chance, give him a chance!"

The man who gave me a chance was Dr. W. H. Snyder, the principal of Hollywood High School. He was kind enough to give me an opportunity and I took it.

When Dr. Snyder left us, the Spanish instructor turned to me and said, "He is a grand old man!" Then he took me to the registrar's office.

The first two weeks in Hollywood High School were very pleasant for me. I always managed to sit next to a pretty girl and carefully planned to walk out of the classroom with one, and quite often with two.

The first day in my roll-call room a boy in an army uniform spoke to me and asked, "What is your name?'

"Luis Pérez," I answered.

"Louise?"

"Yes."

"But that is a girl's name."

"No, in Spanish my name is spelled L-u-i-s, and sounds the same as the name used for the American girls."

"That is funny—you should change it. I will call you Louie, for short." After some conversation he asked, "Louie, why don't you join the R.O.T.C., and learn to be a soldier? You will wear a uniform like me and you will save your 'civvies.'"

"What do you mean by R.O.T.C.?"

"It means Reserve Officers Training Corps. If you wish to join us I can take you to the office."

During one of my free periods the soldier boy took me to the army office, and there he saluted the captain, saying, "Sir, I got another candidate for the company."

"Good work, soldier," said the commander. "Take him to the sergeant to get his uniform."

"Yes, sir," saluted the cadet again; then he took me to the supply room. Here another R.O.T.C. boy issued me an army blouse, a pair of trousers, two woolen shirts, a black necktie, two belts, a cap, and a pair of leggings. When I had my uniform in my arms the sergeant called me and said, "Son, you come here and sign these papers."

"Yes, sir," I replied.

"What is your name?"

I told him my name.

"What is your nationality?"

"Mexican."

"Are you a citizen of the United States?"

"No, sir," I said.

"Son, we can't do anything for you. You have to be an American citizen before you can join the army. You'd better take the uniform back."

"What can I do to become an American citizen?" I asked.

"If you want to be naturalized, go to the Los Angeles Post Office and take out your first papers, and when you have them we can enlist you in the R.O.T.C. Good-by, son."

That afternoon I went to the Los Angeles Post Office, and within five minutes the clerk of the immigration department said, "Raise your right hand. 'Do you swear to tell the truth and nothing but the truth, and that these statements you have stated in this document are true to the best of your knowledge, so help you God.'"

"I do."

Then he handed me my first papers and said, "One dollar, please."

I paid my dollar and the next day I was assigned to the Hollywood High School R.O.T.C. band to play third trombone.

The next thing that happened to me during my first week in high school was an unexpected experience as a result of an intelligence test. One day during roll call a large group of students were herded to a study hall. Here several men and women gave out booklets to each one of the students. As the instructors were passing the pamphlets, one of them said, "Don't look at the papers until we tell you to do so." After all of us had the papers on our desks, the head examiner said, "First of all, put your last name first and your roll-call room at the top of your paper. Then, when we tell you, 'Go,' you mark after each statement a plus or a minus sign as the case may be. When we tell you, 'Stop,' do so."

Soon we were at work, and at the end of half an hour of marking plus and minus signs after each statement, the chief examiner shouted, "Stop! Pass your papers to your right, and go back to your classes."

Several days later I was called to one of the classrooms, and one of the people who had given the psychology test to us was in the room alone. When I knocked to attract his attention, he said, "Come in, come in." As I came in he offered me a chair, asking, "Your name is Luis, is it not?"

"Yes, sir."

"What are two times two? Quick, quick!"

"Four, señor."

"Was Christ a carpenter, teacher, philosopher, or a Savior?"

"He was all of them, señor."

"What do you mean by 'sayñor'?"

"'Señor' means 'mister' or 'sir,' señor," I explained.

"Cross your legs," commanded the man.

As I obeyed his command, he took a small, hard rubber mallet out of his pocket. Then he came closer to me and sat down swinging the mallet carelessly. Suddenly he asked, "Where were you born?"

"I was born in Mex—ouch! Why are you doing that to me?" I asked, as I stood holding my knee.

"Don't worry, son. I am only studying reflexes. I hit you below your kneecap to see if you responded like other normal children. The intelligence test that we gave the other day showed that your I.Q. was very low. We thought that we had found a real idiot. But you are normal. You may go. No doubt this error was due to the fact that you do not understand English. Your I.Q. in Spanish might be high. Good-by, young man."

"You are certainly very strange people. You are always speaking in the terms of letters. If I say something to someone, the answer is 'O.K.' or 'I'll be damned if I know.' A boy asked me the other day to join the

R.O.T.C. I have a piece of paper in my pocket which says 'I.O.U. thirty dollars.' Last week I received a package C.O.D., and now you tell me that my I.Q. is very low. What do you mean by I.Q.?"

"Young man, I.Q. means Intelligence Quotient."

"Ah! Okay. Now everything is clear to me. Thank you—good-by, *señor*," I replied. Then I limped to my next class.

37

June twenty-eighth, 1928, was the date set for my graduation and I was very busy. One of my greatest desires was to take my second citizenship papers on or about the same time I would graduate from high school. With that in mind, one day during my 1927 Christmas vacation, I went to the Los Angeles Post Office. In the immigration room a lady clerk came to assist me.

"What is it that you want?" she asked.

"I would like to get my citizenship papers."

"The first ones?"

"No, ma'am, the second ones."

"Have you the first papers with you?"

"Yes, ma'am—here they are." She looked them over and went back to the files, taking the papers with her.

While I was waiting for the clerk to come back from the file room, I saw that there were several other applicants for citizenship papers. In one corner of the room there was a judge examining an old Irishman.

"Mr. O'Neal," the judge asked, "have you read the United States Constitution?"

"Your honor, I'll tell you—I want to be honest with you. The only thing I have red are these few hairs I have in the back of me neck."

After that remark the judge sent Mr. O'Neal to sober up and to study the Constitution of the United States.

After a long wait, the clerk who had my petition came back with a bunch of papers in her hand and questioned me, "Young man, where have you been? We have been looking for you for the last three and a half years."

"Why, I have been attending Hollywood High School. I have stated so in the papers."

"Do you know that you are illegally in the United States?"

"No, ma'am, I do not know."

"Yes, you should have gone back to Mexico a year after you

entered this country."

"What do you think I should do now? I want to get my papers and stay in the United States."

"The only thing I can tell you to do is to get back to Mexico, and enter again, fulfilling all the requirements demanded by the laws of the United States. After you have done so, you can take out your first papers again."

"Isn't there any other way this thing can be fixed besides going back to Mexico? You see, I am graduating from high school next summer, and I would like to stay here and go to college."

"There is nothing that I can do for you, but you may go to Room 101 and talk to the immigration inspectors there. They might be able to help and advise you as to what to do in your case."

I thanked the young lady for her information and then went to see the immigration officers. After I had talked to one of the inspectors about my trouble, he said, "The only thing you can do that might possibly help is to fill in these papers." He gave me several legal forms all clipped together and continued, "Get two passport photographs and a twenty-dollar money order addressed to the Immigration Department, Washington, D. C. Then bring everything to me and I will see what I can do for you."

The printed matter on the authorized paper was so complicated that I had to pay two dollars and fifty cents to a notary public to help me answer the questions.

The next day I took the money order, the photographs, and the documents to the immigration inspector. After he had looked everything over and took my fingerprints, he said, "Now all you have to do is to wait until we send for you. If you change your address, let us know."

"How long will it take for my papers to come back?" I asked.

"Oh—probably from three to six months—sometimes a little longer."

"And after I get these papers back, will I be a citizen of the United States?"

"No. You will get a small card stating that you have entered the United States legally according to the law provided and approved by

Congress."

Since there was nothing else to do, I thanked the inspector for his help and went back to my school to await developments.

38

The twenty-eighth day of June, 1928, I received my diploma from Hollywood High School, and by the beginning of the following school year I was enrolled at one of the universities of Los Angeles, studying to become a teacher and teach my American friends the language of Cervantes. While in college as a regular student I was fortunate in obtaining a school janitor job, which paid sixty-five dollars per month.

Soon after entering college, I received a small green card from the United States Immigration Department with the following inscription:

Original CERTIFICATE OF REGISTRY Form No. 658
No. 3446 U.S. DEPARTMENT OF LABOR
IMMIGRATION SERVICE

This is to certify that the registry of entry into the United States of the alien whose name and description appears on the reverse hereof has been made as provided in section I and III of an act of Congress approved March 2, 1929.

Date of issue—March 10, 1930.

With said card in my pocket I proceeded to apply for my citizenship papers, but I was informed by the immigration clerk that under the laws of the United States I had to wait from two to five years before getting the final papers. So again, while waiting, I went back to the university.

One afternoon of the same year a Mexican friend of mine, who was very prominent among the Mexican people of Los Angeles, sent me an invitation to celebrate the Cinco de Mayo, which is one of the Mexican Independence Days. The card stated: *"Señor* Pérez: The Mexican

Association of Los Angeles, California, invites you to attend a picnic at Griffith Park, to celebrate the 68th anniversary of the independence of Mexico from the French, the 5th of May, 1862. You are requested to dress in a Mexican costume."

I was pleased to receive the invitation, and at the appointed day I was proudly dressed in a *Charro* suit, sitting under a California live oak tree, talking to a beautiful Mexican *señorita*.

The celebration consisted of a brilliant display of color, amateur talent, and patriotic speechmaking. There was plenty of free food and drink for all.

Dolores Ramirez, the *señorita* to whom I had been properly introduced, was richly dressed in a *China Poblana* costume. Her skirt was full and wide, made of vivid red and green silk, luxuriously embroidered with flat beads. The blouse she wore was of fine white cloth, also embroidered. She wore a wide-brimmed Mexican sombrero and a pair of green slippers. A silk scarf carelessly hung over her shoulders. Her neck displayed an expensive necklace. Her wrists were covered with becoming antique bracelets. On her ears hung magnificent, delicately engraved gold earrings. She was very friendly toward everybody, and a bit flirtatious. Once she said, "Luis, I must see you more often—I would like to know you better."

"Why?" I asked.

"Because I would like to know why you were so indifferent toward me this morning."

"No, Dolores, I was not indifferent. I was just cautious."

"Cautious of what?"

"Of beautiful *señoritas* such as you."

She laughed heartily and as she was doing so, she saw a large bird's nest on top of the oak. Right away she exclaimed, "I want that nest." Then she said, "Luis, will you climb and get it for me, please? I'm making a collection of nests."

I obliged the *señorita*, and while I was scaling the rough tree a crowd of men, women, and children gathered around the place shouting, whistling, and making remarks concerning my clumsy way of climbing. Finally I reached the nest, and when I was about to get it, out crawled an enormous black snake, sticking out his tongue at me. I was so frightened that I lost my balance and dropped down, breaking off some branches as I fell, and also fracturing my collarbone as I hit the ground in an unconscious heap.

I regained consciousness while I was being rushed to the Hollywood Receiving Hospital, where, besides being treated for minor lacerations on the face, limbs, and body, I was supplied with a temporary splint to brace my fractured collarbone. Dolores felt very bad about what had happened. She blamed herself for the accident. On the other hand, I was somewhat glad of the unpredicted turn of events because I became better acquainted with her through her daily visits during my convalescence period, which lasted over a week. After I was well again, I resumed my studies at the university, and went back to my routine work, but I continued to see Dolores frequently.

Once during the latter part of my last semester a the college, I went to visit her, and upon seeing me she said, "Luis, I am so happy that I can shout with joy."

"What is the reason for your happiness, Dolores?" I asked.

"My papa told me that I may go to visit my aunt in Mexico City. I am going to be away for about six months. Isn't that wonderful?"

"Yes, Dolores, it is, but—"

"But what?" she interrupted me.

"Dolores, I was going to ask you to be my wife, but now I—"

"Were you, my adorable idiot?" she said, interrupting me again and grasping my hand.

"Yes."

"It is about time, but I don't think I can give you definite answer until I come back from Mexico."

"I can wait until then, but no longer," I said, as she proceeded to tell me all about her plans.

After a long talk we concluded our conversation with the understanding that I was to take her to the station in my car the next day, which was the date of her departure.

Outside her house that night, as I was telling her good-by under the romantic California moon, she said, "Luis, if you are able to talk to God, ask Him to bring me back to California safe and sound."

"I will," I said, as she placed her quivering lips on mine, and then hurried away.

The next afternoon I took my Dolores to the bus station, and soon she was on her way to Mexico. Upon leaving she said, "I will write often, God willing."

On the way back to my room I stopped at the Pershing Square Park to look at the scenery. While there I met a swarthy Mexican, who spoke to me in broken English. "*Señor*," he said, "my name ees Pablo Calderon, and my wife shee ees agoeen' to have one babee, I theenk. Shee wanta leetle cheecken for her for to eat, I theenk. You geeve me feeftee centavos, please, for to buy one for shee, eh?"

"Why don't you speak to me in Spanish?" I asked in my native language. "I am a Mexican."

At that remark his face brightened, but at the same time he remained with his mouth half open, gazing at me with awe. Finally he asked in his same atrocious English, "Why didn' you told mee, beefore I espoka the Engleesh?"

"Because you did not give me a chance to tell you," I said, handing him the fifty cents.

As the man took the money, he bowed humbly, hat in hand, and said, "*Dios se lo pague, amigo.*" Then repeating the same thing in broken English, he continued,

"May God repay you, friend of mine, and I hope my babee weel be as kind as you are."

"Thank you," I replied. "Here take this other fifty cent piece and if your baby is a boy, name him Luis after me."

For some reason or other my new friend continued murdering the King's English and misusing personal pronouns. On taking the second coin, he shrugged his shoulders, and said pathetically, "But, *señor*, what eef hee ees one shee?"

"Then you may name her Dolores, after my—"

"Dolores, after your mama, eh, *señor*?" he interrupted me.

"No, my friend, name her Dolores after my sweetheart."

"Good, good, I have the name for my babee, and one dola' for two cheecken for the wife, I theenk," he mumbled to himself. Then bowing, he continued, "Goor-by Don Luis, eef my babee shee ees one tree I name heen Luis, for you, *señor*, but eef my babee hee ees one she I name her Dolores for your sweetheart, no?"

"*Sí*," I answered, hoping to get him back to using Spanish.

As he put on his sombrero I heard him mutter to himself. Then raising his arm and waving, he said, "Goor-by, *señor*, I onderstan', I theenk. My papa, he use' to told mee I was one luckee *hombre*. Goor-by, *señor*."

"Good-by, *amigo*," I shouted, then went to my room to rest.

A few days later, after I had gone to the post office to apply for my second citizenship papers, I went to the Mexican plaza. While I was there, feeding popcorn to the birds, the same Mexican tapped the back of my shoulder, and as I turned, he addressed me in his native language, "*Señor*, I named my baby Luis, but the little one only lived three days. He died—may he soon be in Heaven," he continued, making the sign of the cross.

"I am sorry to hear it, my friend," I said.

"Me too, *señor*," he replied, taking from his hip pocket a double-sized red handkerchief, and wiping his eyes and nose.

"Don't take it so hard, *amigo*, you can always adopt—"

"Yes, *señor*, but the wife she is sorry too," he interrupted.

"Crying will not bring him back," I said, as I put my arm around his shoulder and asked him to take a ride with me. He accepted and we went. As I, too, was feeling sad because I had to be separated from Dolores, we had something in common.

Later we went to his house where I met Doña Luz, his wife. She was a typical Mexican-Indian, friendly, neat, and a good worker. At the time she was brokenhearted over the death of their child, but she told me that her husband had promised to take her to Yosemite National Park for a short vacation.

I visited my friend Pablo and his wife almost every day. We talked of many things, including my love for Dolores. Once, about five months after I met him, I went to his house and told him that I was going to take a month's vacation. Immediately he smiled and said, "Ah, Luis, you can take me and Luz to Yosemite Park. We can hunt, hike, and fish there, yes, no?"

After a moment of consideration I said, "Yes, Pablo, we'll go, but first we must get plenty of food."

"*Sí, sí*," he mumbled, rushing to look for his hat, after which we went to town and made what purchases we needed.

Two days later, with plenty of beans, rice, canned goods, and coffee in my car, Pablo, his wife, and I found ourselves on the way to Yosemite National Park. There we spent a happy month's vacation fishing, hunting, hiking, and resting.

39

The day Pablo and I returned from Yosemite I found a lot of correspondence from Dolores, and in one of her letters she told me that she was coming home Wednesday, December 12—the following Wednesday. She asked me to meet her at the Los Angeles bus station at three o'clock in the afternoon. On Monday, the day after we had returned from our vacation, I received a letter from the United States Department of Labor advising me to appear in the immigration office, December 12, at ten o'clock, to be sworn in by a court judge to receive my certificate of citizenship. That news made me so happy that immediately I went out and bought a new suit for the occasion.

On Wednesday morning, as I was preparing to leave for the Post Office, I received a telegram from Dolores which read:

DEAR LUIS STOP SCHEDULE CHANGED STOP

WILL ARRIVE TODAY WEDNESDAY DECEMBER 12TH AT ELEVEN THIRTY AM INSTEAD OF THREE PM STOP MEET ME AT GREYHOUND STATION WITHOUT FAIL STOP WILL GIVE YOU A DEFINITE ANSWER TO THE QUESTION WHICH YOU ASKED THE NIGHT BEFORE I LEFT LOS ANGELES STOP DOLORES.

Dolores's telegram made me so happy that for a moment I did not know what to do. I was happy beyond words. She was coming the same day on which I was to get my final citizenship papers, which represented one of my very greatest desires. And the last line of her telegram aroused my hopes so high that I went down stairs and kissed the landlady. Also I handed a dollar tip to the garbage collector, who happened to be on his route as I stepped out the door on my way to get my car to go to the Federal Building.

At ten-thirty, Wednesday, December 12, at the Los Angeles Post Office, I was conducted to a large room where a court judge gave me a very rigid examination on the Constitution of the United States. Upon completing the verbal inquiry I was led to another room where a second judge administered to me the oath of allegiance to the American Government. From the second courtroom I was taken to the immigration office, where the clerk in charge said, "Raise your right hand." When I had my arm in the air, he chanted, "Do you solemnly swear that the statements you have made are, to the best of your knowledge, the truth, the whole truth, and nothing but the truth—so help you God?"

"Yes, I do."

"Ten dollars, please," he said, handing me the pen to sign the papers.

After, I had paid my fee, he added, "Mr. Pérez, we will send your certificate of citizenship to you soon. I hope you will become an outstanding citizen of the United States, and will enjoy the privileges and protection which this country extends to every person who, by choice, has sworn allegiance to the Government, the Flag, and the Constitution. Good-by, and good luck."

At the end of his speech I shook hands with him and left. At the door, a jovial, fat, colored guard patted my shoulder and said, "Congratulations, mistah, now you is an American citizen. Yeah, suh—you is one of us."

When I stepped out of the building I happened to glance to the right, and high on top of the steel mast the flag of my newly adopted country proudly waved with the breeze. As I beheld it, I stood motionless in a gesture of reverence. Then, after performing a military salute, I walked fast to the parking lot, got into my car, and drove to the bus station to meet Dolores.

On my way to the station I said to myself, "If Dolores will say 'yes' to my question, that will be the climax of a perfect today, and the beginning of a new tomorrow."